A GALAXY OF HISTORICAL AND CULTURAL ATTRACTIONS IN THE CITY OF GUANGZHOU
广州历史文化名城荟萃

主　　编：陶诚、张嘉极
副 主 编：赵清木、温朝晖、邓扬威（执行）
责任编辑：钟萍
特约编辑：张任
策划撰文：邓扬威
摄影设计：见山、闻克峰、何勇当、郑振钦、陈爱珍等

EDITORS-IN-CHIEF: TAO CHENG, ZHANG JIA-JI
DEPUTY EDITORS-IN-CHIEF: ZHAO QING-MU, WEN ZHAO-HUI,
DENG YANG-WEI (EXECUTIVE EDITOR)
EXECUTIVE EDITOR: ZHONG PING
GUEST EDITOR: ZHANG REN
PLANNER AND WRITER: DENG YANG-WEI
PHOTOGRAPHING DESIGNERS: JIAN SHAN, WEN KE-FENG, HE YONG-DANG,
ZHENG ZHEN-XIN, CHEN AI-ZHEN

廣東旅游出版社

图书在版编目（CIP）数据

广州历史文化名城荟萃/广州市文化局编. ——广州：广东旅游出版社，2004.12
ISBN 7-80653-615-9

Ⅰ.广… Ⅱ.广… Ⅲ.广州市-概况 Ⅳ.K926.51

中国版本图书馆 CIP 数据核字（2004）第 136308 号

责任编辑：钟　萍
装帧设计：见　山
封面设计：明　镜
责任技编：顾耀民

广东旅游出版社出版发行
（广州市中山一路 30 号之一　邮编：510600）
深圳市普加彩印务有限公司印刷
(深圳市龙华创艺路亿康工业园B座)
广东旅游出版社图书网
www.tourpress.cn
邮购地址：广州市中山一路 30 号之一
联系电话：020-87347871　87347732　邮编：510600
889×1194 毫米　20 开　6 印张　20 千字
2007 年第 1 版第 4 次印刷
印数：5701-6000 册
定价：35.00 元

本书如有错页倒装等质量问题，请直接与印刷厂联系换书。

前　言

　　广州北控五岭，近扼三江，得天独厚的山水环境造就了这座美丽的城市，养育了世世代代的广州人。

　　广州集中原精粹，纳四海新风，为中华民族增辉：开拓"海上丝绸之路"；打响中国人民反抗英国侵略斗争的"第一枪"，成为近代中国革命策源地；改革开放一马当先，经济发展迅速，市场发育比较成熟，经济实力名列前茅……

　　悠悠岁月，沧海桑田，建城于公元前214年的广州，是国家历史文化名城，历史文化遗存极为丰富。发挥这些珍贵遗产在广东建设文化大省、广州建设文化强市中的作用，是《广州历史文化名城荟萃》画册编辑出版的主要目的。我们力图以直观、感性的方式，使读者真实地、全面地认识广州的历史文化，尽量减少甚至完全摒弃许多同类书籍所具有的"繁文缛节"，开门见山，使读者能得到更多实质性的文化信息和内容。如本书开篇，就仅用几百字前言来代替历史图册中惯常的万言序文；又如除目录外，全书中不再设专门的栏目页；大部分图片都不加累赘的说明以防破坏视觉效果，等等。我们所有的努力，都是希望一向予读者古老、沉闷印象的历史文化能够在书中真正感性起来、鲜活起来，以适应如今这个"读图时代"，适应口味不断变化着的读者，使更多的人对广州的历史文化感兴趣，从而参与到名城广州的历史文化保护和"文化强市"的建设中来。

　　本书图片中的名城资源，属于大家比较熟悉的，摄影者就力求以新的角度、以细节来加以反映；属于大家不熟悉但有相当价值的，摄影者就设法寻找出来，通过有代表性的镜头为读者奉上。不过限于篇幅，对于很多同样是十分珍贵的历史文化遗存，本书未能够一一录入，这是比较可惜的事情。这遗憾只能等时机成熟，在本书再版的时候加以弥补了。

　　在本书的编辑出版过程中，我们参考了《广州百科全书》、《名城广州小百科》、《旅游在中国——广州》、《中国100名城》、《广州》、《广州名城辞典》、《辉煌的广州》等文献资料，得到了名城办、有关景观景点、有关单位和个人在资料稿件提供、协助拍摄、历史考证等方面的大力支持，在此一并致以衷心的谢意。

● 编者 ●

FOREWORD

Guangzhou is adjacent to the five ridges (the area covering Guangdong and Guangxi provinces) to the north and also near the 3 rivers. Thanks to the God-given natural environment, Guangzhou has been endued with a picturesque scene to live in.

Over many years in the past, Guangzhou has made a perfect fusion of different cultures from across the country, and polished its name by means of a series of brilliant accomplishments: origin place of the marine silk road, the very first base of the Chinese people with regard to fighting against British invaders, the pilot player in implementing the country's policy of reform and opening-up, speedy economic growth, hosting of a better development market economy, and solid economic strengths which rank it on the top of the list among other cities in China……

Founded as early as in B.C. 214, the city of Guangzhou has been known to host a hoard of historical and cultural attractions. This picture album is published and released for the main purpose to highlight these precious relics for the good of building Guangdong province to be one of the major cultural attractions in the country, and allowing Guangzhou to embrace quicker developments through cultural inspiration. We do our utmost to enable readers to have a visual experience of the historical and culture scenes in Guangzhou in a comprehensive way. In the literal description paragraphs, we stick to a concise and right-to-the-point pattern of introduction, in order to allow readers to have access to more substantial cultural information at a glance. For an example, we write only a few hundred characters in the Introduction to enlighten the readers as to what their eyes are to savor; for another example, except for the Table of Contents, we offer no other "A Glance of Columns" pages. Furthermore, we do not attach complicated literal annotations to pictures, thus to avoid affecting the visual effects of all these impressive pictures. We did all this in a hope of providing readers with quite a pleasant and agreeable reading experience, to enliven historical culture, which was traditionally thought to be archaic and boring, to adjust to the changing taste of readers in this picture-reading era, so that more and more people would become interested in the historical and cultural traditions of Guangzhou, before contributing their efforts to the city's drive for protecting its historical and cultural relics and embracing quicker developments through the promotion of cultural activities. Photographers have resorted to a creative and brand-new perspective and tried to reveal the inherent character of the city in great detail; they strove also for presenting readers all those attractions, which are not well acquainted by the general public, but of considerable values. We wish that we had more space and time to present a longer list of pictures featuring the historical and cultural relics; and we hope to add in as many as possible into the new version, which is expected to emerge soon. During the editing and publishing course, we have referred to the "Cyclopedia of Guangzhou", "A Brief Cyclopedia of the Renowned City of Guangzhou", "Travel in China——Guangzhou" "Top 100 Cities of Fame in China", "Inside Guangzhou" "All about Guangzhou", and "Guangzhou, City of Splendor", and other literatures and data; we have also received generous supports and assistance from the "City Image Improvement Office", Managerial Authorities of related sites and relics, related organizations and individuals, in terms of data/information sourcing, photographing, textual research upon historical information; we would like to extend our heart-felt thanks to each and every person who have helped us.

● EDITOR ●

CATALOG 目录

Cultural Relics	文物景观	1-39
Religious Sites	宗教遗存	40-56
Academic Premises	书院场馆	57-65
Ancient Villages	古 村 寨	66-72
Historical Remains of Personages	名人遗迹	73-87
Latter-day Historical Relics	近代史迹	88-107
Folk Customs	民俗风情	108-109
Arts of Ling-nan Style	岭南艺术	110-113
Businesses with Time-honored Reputation	老 字 号	114

A GALAXY OF HISTORICAL AND CULTURAL ATTRACTIONS IN THE CITY OF GUANGZHOU

七星岗古海岸遗址
Relics of Ancient Coast at 7-Star Hillock

位于石榴岗，1937年中山大学地理系教授吴尚时发现。它表明远古时南海水域深入到珠三角的北部，突破了世界古海岸线与今天海岸线宽度最大值50千米的说法。

Nestled in the Pomegranate Hillock, and found by Wu Shang-shi, professor in the Department of Geography with Zhong-shan University in 1937. It indicated that in ancient times, the water in the South China Sea ever wound through the northern part of the Pearl River Delta region, and thus constituted a breakthrough into the saying that "the maximum width between the ancient coastline and the coastline in the present-day world is 50 kilometers".

文物景观

飞鹅岭新石器遗址
Relics of the Neolithic Age at the Flying Goose Hill

位于华南植物园，距今2200-4000年。20世纪50年代出土了石斧、石锛等磨制石器；夔纹、云雷纹等陶片；陶纺轮、陶网坠、玉环、玉块等物品并发现了大片烧土层。

Nestled in the South China Botanical Garden, aged between 2,200-4,000 years so far. In 1950s, some grinding-purpose stone implements, such as stone zax and stone adz, were excavated in here; whilst other articles as a result of excavation work here included: pottery tiles bearing the shapes of a one-legged monster, clouds or thunderbolt; figuline spinning wheels, figuline net pendents, jade rings and blocks, etc. besides, large pieces of roasted soil layers were also excavated.

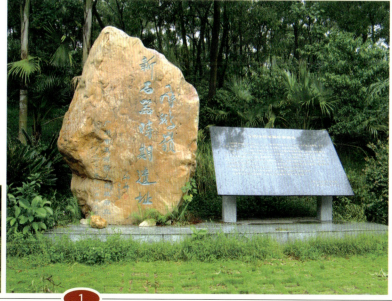

西汉南越王墓博物馆
The Western Han Dynasty Mausoleum of the Nan-yue King

位于解放北路,是南越开国之君赵佗的孙子,即第二代南越王赵眜的陵墓,是岭南地区年代最早的一座大型彩绘石室墓。其出土的丝缕玉衣、"文帝行玺"金印和"赵眜"玉印,以及1000多件(套)精美珍贵的玉器、青铜器等随葬品,被誉为"岭南文化之光"和"国宝"。

Nestled in Jie-fang-bei Road. Nan-yue King was the grandson of the Founder of the Nan-yue Empire, Zhao Tuo. This is the mausoleum of the second Nan-yue King named Zhao Mei, being the earliest excavated mastaba housing a galaxy of colored paintings in the Ling-nan Area. The silk thread clothes adorned with jewels, "Wen Emperor's Imperial Seal" made of gold and "Zhao Mei's Stamp made of Jade", and over 1,000 pieces (sets) of finely-made and precious jade articles and bronze funerary objects are seen as the "Splendor of Ling-nan Style Culture" and "National Treasure".

文物景观

镇海楼
Zhen-hai Tower

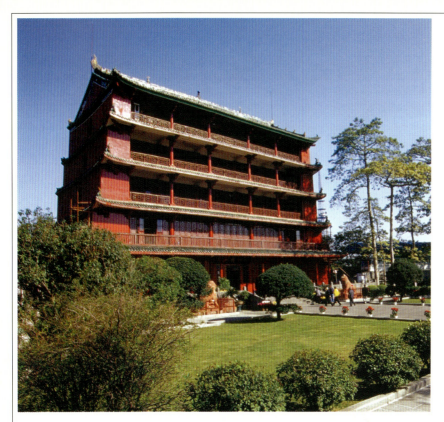

位于越秀山上,又名望海楼,俗称五层楼,建于明洪武十三年,清代羊城八景之一,被誉为"五岭以南第一楼"、"岭南第一胜览",历来是登临览胜之地,其图案被广泛用作广州的标志。镇海楼现为广州博物馆,常年展出《广州历史陈列》以及广州地区的考古发掘和文物收集所得。下右图为楼前的石狮子。

Nestled on the Yue-xiu Mount, alternatively termed as The Sea-Viewing Tower, and known by the general public as the 5-Storey Tower. Constructed in the 13th year of Hong-wu Emperor of Ming Dynasty, listed as one of the Eight Attractions of Guangzhou in Qing Dynasty. Famed as the No.1 Tower to the south of the 5 Ridges, it is the No.1 Attraction in Guangdong and Guangxi Provinces. It has been regarded as a tourist attraction over many years. Its pattern has been widely used as a symbol of Guangzhou. Nowadays, Zhen Hai Tower has become the home of Guangzhou Museum, where the "Exhibition of Historical Relics in Guangzhou" was launched and those objects and cultural relics excavated as a result of archaeological operations are displayed throughout the entire year. The lower picture on the right shows the stone lions at the gate of the tower.

文物景观

南越国宫署遗址
Site of the Imperial Palace of Nan-yue Empire

位于中山四路,有宫署走道、御花园、地下石构建筑、水井、水渠等,是目前我国仅见的汉代宫署花园实例,极为珍贵。

Nestled in Zhong-shan No. 4 Road, hosts imperial passageways, royal gardens, underground stone structures, water wells, and canals, etc. This is deemed as the only and a highly precious imperial garden designed in a Han Dynasty style, in today's China.

文物景观

粤王井
Yue King Well

位于连新路,广州现存最古老的井。相传是赵佗所掘,王府专用。《广州府志》称:"佗饮斯水,肌体润泽,年百余岁,视听不衰"。

Nestled in Lian-xin Road, the oldest well in Guangzhou so far. Said to be sunk by Zhao Tuo and used solely by the royal family. According to the "Annals of Guangzhou", "Zhao Tuo drinks water taken from this well, and finds that the water here can nourish his skin and prolong his life, as well as improve his eyesight and sense of hearing.

南汉德陵遗址
Site of Southern Han De Mausoleum

位于小谷围岛，俗称"刘王冢"。陵墓规模较大，有可能是岭南第二个地方王朝的陵寝。据有关专家推断，此墓为南汉国奠基者刘隐的陵墓。据《资治通鉴》等文献记述，刘隐死后，其弟刘岩称帝，追尊为襄帝，墓号为德陵。上图为德陵航拍，中图为墓圹填土解剖，下图为墓中陶瓷。

Nestled on the Xiao-gu-wei Island, normally called "Liu Wang Tomb". Covers a relatively large area, and said to be the second excavated mausoleum of the ancient local empire in Guangdong and Guangxi provinces. According to some experts, this is the tomb of Liu Yin, the founder of Nan-han Empire. As stated in "Comprehensive mirror to aid in government" and other literatures, after Liu Yin died, his younger brother Liu Yan succeeded to the throne, and granted a title "Xiang King" to Liu Yin and dedicated Liu Yin's tomb as a "mausoleum of a man of good virtues". The upper picture is a photo taken of the mausoleum from the air, the middle picture shows the earth-filling and anatomizing operations in the tomb, and the lower picture shows the ceramics found in the tomb.

文物景观

南汉康陵遗址
Relics of Nan-han Kang Mausoleum

位于小谷围,据墓中哀册文称,此为南汉高祖刘岩的陵墓。据清康熙二十五年《番禺县志》和屈大均《广东新语》等记载,康陵在明崇祯九年遭大规模盗扰。墓中完整器极少。上图为康陵全景,中图为墓室内景,下图为保存得较完整的陶制水果。

Nestled on the Xiao-gu-wei Island. As stated in the eulogy leaflet found inside, this is the tomb of Liu Yan, the Gao-zu Emperor of Nan-han Empire. According to the statements in the "Annals of Panyu County" dated the 25th year of Kang-xi Emperor Reign and the "New Annals of Guangdong" by Qu Da-jun, the Kang Mausoleum was massively looted in the 9th year of Chong-zhen Emperor's Reign in the Ming Dynasty. Few objects in the tomb still remain unbroken. The upper picture shows a bird's view of the mausoleum, the middle picture is the interior scene in the tomb, and the lower picture shows the figuline fruits that remain in relatively good condition.

文物景观

传统中轴线
Traditional axis line

广州市第一批历史文化保护区之一。广州古城核心区域在历史上形成了"六脉皆通海，青山半入城"的城市传统中轴线：从越秀山中山纪念碑往南经中山纪念堂——市府合署大楼——人民公园——海珠广场并向江南大道延伸。越秀山中山纪念碑到海珠桥北端的距离约2350米。传统中轴线奠定了旧城格局，本身又是一个大景观，在线上及周边分布的文物古迹和旅游景点众多，广州旧城中心区现存的古树名木大多分布在这一地带，是十分宝贵的旅游资源。

文物景观

Among the first group of protected sites for historical and cultural values in Guangzhou. The core area of the ancient city of Guangzhou has featured a formation of an axis line, which extends from the Zhong-shan Monument at the food of Yue-xiu Mount southward to Zhong-shan Memorial Hall to the City Hall, then to the People's Park, Hai-zhu Square and then to Jiang-nan Avenue. The distance from the Zhong-shan Monument at the food of Yue-xiu Mount to the northern end of Hai-zhu Bridge is approximately 2,350 meters. The traditional axis line has defined the layout of the ancient city of Guangzhou. Actually, the areas that this axis line have hosted a hoard of scenic spots and cultural attractions. On top of that, most of those famed and ancient trees living in the city of Guangzhou are located in this area, and are rather precious tourist resources.

传统中轴线
Traditional axis line

说明：上图为北京路步行街，中图为广州解放纪念碑，下图为珠江夜景。

Notes: The upper picture shows the Foot Path in Beijing Road, the middle picture shows Guangzhou Liberation Monument, and the lower picture shows the night view on Pearl River.

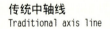

文物景观

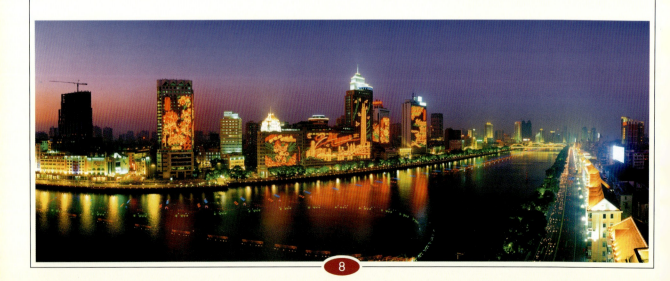

白云山
White Clouds Mount

广州市第一批历史文化保护区之一，位于广州市区北面，因峰顶常有白云飘绕而得名，是构成广州依山傍水城市主要因素之一。其森林植被有净化城市空气的关键作用，有广州"市肺"之称。其"白云晚望"、"景泰僧归"、"蒲涧濂泉"、"白云松涛"、"云山锦绣"等为宋代以来各时期的羊城八景之一。山中寺庙、景点众多，留下了历代许多名人的足迹。

Among the first group of protected sites for historical and cultural values in Guangzhou. Nestled to the north of the downtown area of Guangzhou. Named after the fact that white clouds always pervade its peak. Constitutes a major element in the "landscaped image" of Guangzhou. The forest vegetation is able to purify the air in the city; thus the Mount is called the "lung of Guangzhou". The mount is renowned for quite a few great scenic attractions, which have been listed among the "Eight Major Scenes in Guangzhou". Besides, there are a number of temples and scenic spots in the mount, as well as relics of many personages.

文物景观

文物景观

白云山
White Clouds Mount

说明：左上图为天南第一峰牌坊，右上图为九龙泉，下图为将军坟。

Notes: the upper picture on the left shows the Memorial Archway at the Tian-Nan No.1 Peak, the upper picture on the right shows the 9-dragon spring, while the lower picture shows the Tomb of a General.

"古之楚庭"牌坊
"Ancient Pavilion by Sunset" Memorial Archway

位于越秀山南麓,兴建于清朝顺治元年。坊额东西两面均有篆体文字石刻,东面为"粤秀奇峰",西面为"古之楚亭",历史上羊城八景点之一。

Nestled at the southern foot of Yue-xiu Mount, initially constructed at the first year of the Shun-zhi Emperor's Reign in Qing Dynasty. On the eastern and western sides of the horizontal tablet, there are inscriptions in seal characters. To the east and west of this archway, there exist two scenic attractions, which are respectively known as the "Astonishing Hills", and the "Ancient Pavilion by Sunset", which were both ever listed among the eight major scenic attractions in the city of Guangzhou.

文物景观

千年古道
Millennial Ancient Path

位于北京路商业步行街。它揭开了层层叠叠的十一层路面,由上而下分属民国、明代、宋元、南汉、唐代等历史时期,此处还发现了五层拱北楼的建筑基址遗址。

It is located in the commercial pedestrian mall of Beijing Road. It unearths the eleven-layer tier upon tier of road surface, which belongs to such historical periods as Republic of China, Ming Dynasty, Song Dynasty, Yuan Dynasty, South Han, Tang Dynasty etc. from top to bottom respectively. In addition, the construction base relic of the five-floor Gongbei Tower is also found.

莲花山
Lotus Mount

广州市第一批历史文化保护区之一,位于狮子洋水道,有山峰40余座,其主要景观中的莲花塔原名文昌塔,高九层,雄踞江口,外来船舶以此为航标,故有"省会华表"之称;莲花古城始建于清康熙三年六月,作哨所之用,为防范明将郑成功进攻东南沿海,鸦片战争时曾设防,稍后琦善与英军义律在此城密议"穿鼻草约";莲花山古采石场遗址占地500余亩。据考证南越王墓的石料即取自于此。古代石工采石遗留下来的崖洞、潭、壑、凿痕累累构成奇特景观。

Among the city's first group of protected areas for historical and cultural values. Nestled in the Lion Sea Waterway, hosts over 400 hills. Among others, the major scenic spot, Lotus Tower, was originally called Wen-chang Tower, which is a 9-storeyed structure. The Lotus Tower stays at the mount of the local river, and is deemed as a navigation mark by incoming vessels. Thus, it is alternatively called an "Ornamental Column of the Capital City of Guangdong Province". The Ancient City of Lotus was initially constructed in June of the 3rd year of Kang-xi Emperor Reign of Qing Dynasty, and was used as a watchtower at the start. In order to prevent Zheng Cheng-gong, a general with Ming Dynasty, from attacking the cities in the southeastern area of the country, defences were always mounted at this Tower; later, Qi Shan and the British Corps negotiated upon the "Chuan Bi Draft Covenant" by stealth in here. The relics of the ancient quarry at Lotus Mount cover a land area of over 500 mu. According to the findings of archaeological exploration, the stone materials used in the mausoleum of Nan-yue King were exactly taken from this quarry. In here, your eyes will savor an array of sandstone cave, ponds, gullies and chisel marks left by quarrying operations in ancient times.

文物景观

说明:上图为莲花塔远眺,中左图为莲花古城,下左图为古采石场,下右图为望海观音像。

Notes: the upper picture shows a bird's view of the Lotus Tower, the middle picture on the left shows the ancient city of lotus, the lower picture on the left shows the ancient quarry, and the lower picture on the right shows the Figure of Sea-viewing Kwan-yin.

药洲遗址
Relics of Peony Flowers Islet

位于教育路,横匾"药洲"为米芾所题。五代南汉时刘䶮割据岭南,建都广州,此处经开凿成行宫湖沼花园。因地处城西,故称"西湖",又因刘䶮常聚言士于湖洲之上,炼丹求仙药,而洲上遍植红药,故又称"仙湖"、"药洲"。现有关药洲、九曜石以及书院的九十块碑刻,仍嵌廊壁之上。上、下图为药洲园内景致,中图为米芾题写的匾额。

Nestled in Jiao-yu Road; the two Chinese characters "Yao Zhou" on the horizontal tablet were written by Mi Fei. In the Southern Han Period of the ancient Five Dynasties Times, Liu Gong occupied the Ling-nan area of the country (i.e. south of the Five Ridges, the area covering the current Guangdong and Guangxi provinces), and established his own capital in Guangzhou. He ordered workers to set up an imperial palace with a lake and a garden. As the palace is located in the western part of the city, thus the lake was called "West Lake". Later, as Liu Gong often called his advisors to negotiate state affairs on the islet of the lake, and ordered specialists to research the elixir of life; flowers of Chinese harbaceous peony were planted everywhere on the islet; thus, the lake was also called a "fairy lake" or "Peony Flowers Islet". Today, on the islet, there are 90 tablets of inscriptions, which are still mounted on the walls of slypes. The upper picture shows an internal view of the "Peony Flowers Islet" garden, and the middle picture shows the horizontal tablet with the inscription.

文物景观

阿曼航船纪念碑
Omen Sailing Ship Monument

公元8世纪中叶，阿曼航海家奥贝达驾驶一艘双桅木船，辗转颠簸两年后抵达广州，从此拉开了中阿间贸易和文化交流的序幕。阿拉伯文学名著《一千零一夜》中描写海上冒险家辛巴达的故事，就是取材于奥贝达的亲身经历。1980年，为了纪念先辈壮举，阿曼政府建造一艘名为"苏哈尔"号的仿古木船，沿着先人的航迹再访中国。航行了7个半月，木船顺利抵达目的地广州。中阿两国政府高度重视这一盛事，特立碑纪念。上图为纪念碑，下图为碑文。

In the middle period of the 8th century A.D., Aubert, a navigator from Oman, sailed a two-masted wooden vessel, and arrived at Guangzhou after undergoing hardships throughout 2 years, thus blazing a trail for the trading and cultural exchanges between China and Oman. The story of Sinbad, the marine adventurer, in the Arabic literary works "Arabian Nights", was originated exactly from the true happenings on the part of Aubert. In 1980, in order to memorize this feat, the Government of Omen made an ancient-looking wooden vessel called "Sohar", which sailed to arrive in China, along the sailing route of their ancestor. After 7.5 months' sailing, the wooden vessel reached Guangzhou without a hitch. Both the Omen and Chinese governments attached great importance to this event, and jointly erected this monument for memorial purposes. The upper picture shows the monument, and the lower picture shows the inscription on the monument.

石门返照
Stone Door by Back Light

位于石井镇，宋、元两代羊城八景之一。石门有一泉，传说汉后南下广州的官吏多贪污即因饮此泉水，故此泉称为贪泉。贪泉在五代时湮没。晋代广州刺史吴隐之操守廉洁，认为人品与泉水无关，为此赋诗一首："古人云此水，一歃怀千金，试使夷齐饮，终当不易心。"上图为石门夕阳下的景色。

Nestled in the Shi-jing Town, among the 8 major scenic attractions in the Song and Yuan Dynasties. There is a spring at the stone door. As a legend goes, most of those officials who were stationed in Guangzhou and indulged themselves in corruption drank the water in this spring; thus the spring was called "Spring of Greed". The Spring of Greed dried up in the Five Dynasties times. In Jin Dynasty, Wu Yin-zhi, a feudal prefectural governor, impressed the multitude by his probity and integrity. Thus a poem was written especially for him, as memorial ----- "Ancient saying goes that anyone who drinks water from this spring becomes greedy; Let him drink it and it's for sure that his nature won't change a little bit". The upper picture shows the stone door by sunset.

烈女牌坊
Women of Chastity Memorial Archway

皇帝常把殉夫烈女当楷模来张扬。这是位于解放北路,市内不多见的保存完好的烈女牌坊,它见证了封建统治秩序中充满妇女血泪的三纲五常伦理教条。

In ancient times, Chinese emperors often had a relish to disseminate the stories of those women who died in defense of their honor chastity or virginity, thus to educate women to pay utmost allegiance to their husbands. This is a memorial archway for those women of chastity that is rarely seen in Jie-fang Road North, which has witnessed the suffocating rules and code of conduct governing women living in those long-past feudal times.

姑嫂坟
Sisters-in-law Tomb

位于云台花园,建于南宋,坟前有清乾隆四十一年户部尚书梁国治所撰《姑嫂坟碑记》,颂扬姑嫂二人之孝道事迹;姑嫂二人事迹在《番禺县续志》也有记载。

Nestled in the Yun-Tai Park, initially constructed in Southern Song Dynasty. On the gravestone there is an inscription which tells a moving story about two sisters-in-law' filial loyalty to their parents, which was composed by Liang Guo-zhi (a high official with the Board of Revenue and Population) in the 41st year of the Qian-long Emperor Reign of Qing Dynasty. This story has also been included into the "Continued Annals of Panyu County".

文物景观

南园
Southern Park

位于文德路，是元代著名园林。明洪武年间孙蕡、王佐等五人在此创办南园诗社，明嘉靖年间欧大任、梁有誉等在此结成粤山诗社，人称南园后五先生。明崇祯年间陈子壮、黎美周等十二人重开南园诗社。他们在清兵进入广州后大多因不能接受异族的统治而为清兵屠杀。1887年张之洞在这里开广雅书局，刊刻书史经集。1949年后这里改为广东省中山图书馆南馆。图为园景。

Nestled in Wen-de Road, a renowned park constructed in Yuan Dynasty. Sun Fen, Wang Zuo and 3 other persons ever embarked on a "Southern Park Poets Coalition" in here, during the Hong-wu Times of Ming Dynasty. In the Jia-jing times of the Ming Dynasty, 5 persons headed by Ou Da-ren and Liang You-yu set up a "Yu-shan Poets Society", and were later called the "Five Poets of Southern Park". In the Chong-zhen times of the Ming Dynasty, 12 persons headed by Chen Zi-shi and Li Mei-zhou re-opened the Southern Park Poets Society. After the soldiers of the then Qing Dynasty entered the then city of Guangzhou, they were slaughtered for not being willing to accept the ruling by a foreign nationality. In 1887, Zhang Zhi-dong opened a Guang-ya Publishing House in here to have books and scriptures published. After the year 1949, this Park was reconstructed and became the Southern Hall of the Zhong-shan Library of Guangdong Province. The picture shows the scene in the park.

文物景观

留耕堂
Liu-Geng House

位于番禺沙湾,始建于元代,清代重建,距今已有700余年历史,对联中"心田留与后人耕"为堂名由来,1986年辟为"沙湾博物馆"。留耕堂112条木石大柱气势雄伟壮观,最具特色;雕刻和装饰艺术集元、明、清三代之大成,使之成为岭南地区著名的古代乡村祠堂建筑。上图为大牌坊,下图为匾额及大门门神绘画。

Nestled in Sha-wan Town of Panyu District, initially constructed in the ancient Yuan Dynasty, and later reconstructed in Qing Dynasty, which was already more than 700 years old. The House was named after a couplet that is put on its gate. In 1986, this House was expanded to become the "Museum of Sha-wan Town". The House is famed for its 112 large columns made of stone and wood, which look splendid and astonishing. The sculpture and adornment pieces in here are a fusion of authentic styles originated from Yuan, Ming and Qing Dynasties. Hence, this House has already been deemed as a famous structure featuring the typical architectural style of Guangdong and Guangxi provinces. The upper picture shows the big-sized archway gate, and the lower picture shows the horizontal tablet with inscription and the door-god figure.

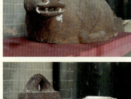

五羊石像
Five-Rams Stone Sculpture

相传有5位仙人骑口衔稻穗的仙羊降临广州，赠谷穗给广州人民，并祝福此地永无饥荒。石像1959年由尹积昌等人设计，现已成为广州标志。

As a legend goes, 5 fairies each rode a ram to arrive at Guangzhou to confer ears of millet to the local people, and wished that this place would never suffer hunger and desolation. The stone sculpture was designed by Yin Ji-chang in 1959, and has now become a symbol of Guangzhou City.

文物景观

Und im Park:
- *Tischtennis*
- *Basketball*
- *Boule-Platz*

V. Five-rans silves zu finder
Tret Boote can see im Park
Viele Kitschfiguren

明城墙
City Wall of Ming Dynasty

图为位于越秀山上的古城墙，是明洪武十三年时永嘉侯朱亮祖组织修建的。其石料大多为凿象岗修北门时所得。

The picture shows the ancient city wall located on the Yue-xiu Mount, which was originally erected by Zhu Liang-zu (a marquis at Yong-jia) in the 13th year of the Hong-wu Times of Ming Dynasty. Most of the stone materials used in the city wall were sourced as a result of the chiseling work at the time when the Northern City Gate was constructed.

琶洲塔
Pa-zhou Tower

位于新港东路，为明代古塔。清代羊城八景之一，称"琶洲砥柱"。塔中有广州罕见的明代石雕。当年周边还建有北帝庙和海鳌寺，现已无存。

Nestled in the Xin-gang-dong Road, an ancient tower erected in Ming Dynasty. Listed as one of the 8 major attractions in Guangzhou in Qing Dynasty. Inside the tower, there exist some rarely seen stone sculptures originated from the Ming Dynasty. In those past years, there always existed the North Emperor Temple and the Sea Turtle Temple, which have been dismantled.

赤岗塔
Chi-gang Tower

位于赤岗，故名。兴建于明万历四十七年，是继琶洲塔、莲花塔之后修建的第三座"风水宝塔"。塔边有托塔力士石刻造像，为明代石刻佳作。

Nestled in the Chi-gang Town, hence its name. Erected in the 47th year of the Wan-li Times of the Ming Dynasty, and considered as the third "Good-Fortune Tower" after the establishment of the Pa-zhou Tower, and the Lotus Tower. By this tower, there exists a sculpture appearing like a strong man who is in a position to support this bridge. This sculpture was a famed work-piece of its own in Ming Dynasty.

通福桥
Tong-fu Bridge

位于石围塘,俗称为五眼桥(广州人称洞为眼),由李待问捐建于明万历年间,距今已300多年,历史上为省佛大道第一桥,是交通要道。
Nestled in Shi-wei-tang, and normally termed as "5-eye Bridge" (people in Guangzhou call a hole in the structure of a bridge as an eye). This bridge was erected by use of money donated by Li Dai-wen in the Wan-Li times of the Ming Dynasty, which was over 300 years ago from toady. This bridge has been the first ever bridge linking Guangzhou and Foshan, being a main traffic artery.

文物景观

毓灵桥
Yu-ling Bridge

位于芳村冲口,是古老的梁式石桥。建桥时间一说为明代,一说为清道光年间。桥名毓灵乃因历史上这里称钟秀乡,取其"钟灵毓秀"之意。
Nestled at the mouth of the branch of the Pearl River in Fang-cun District. An ancient beam type bridge. Some said this bridge was erected in Ming Dynasty, others said in the Dao-guang Emperor Reign of Qing Dynasty. The bridge was named Yu-ling (which means a host of talented people in Chinese language), for the local region has housed a galaxy of wise personages.

21

云桂桥
Yun-Gui Bridge

位于晓港公园，兴建于明朝嘉靖年间，为当年与海瑞齐名的清官何维柏所建。何因弹劾宰相严嵩"怀奸蠹国"而被廷杖削职，归故里时为便民筑此桥。

Nestled in the Xiao-gang Park, and originally built up in the Jia-jing Emperor's Reign of the ancient Ming Dynasty, according to an order given by He Wei-bo, a state official who was as famed for his probity as Hai Rui at the same era. He Wei-bo was removed from his office for his impeachment against the then ill-minded Prime Minister Yan Gao, and sent back to his hometown. His countrymen erected this bridge to commemorate him.

文物景观

文塔
Wen Tower

位于龙津西路，据说建于明末清初。文塔供奉掌握文人骚客功名命运的文曲星。传说文曲星手执一笔，谁被点中便可获功名。所以塔外观酷似一支笔，塔也称"功名塔"。

Nestled in Long-jin Road West, said to be originally built up between the late times of Ming Dynasty and the early times of Qing Dynasty. This tower was constructed to offer sacrifice to the Wen-qu Star, which was believed to take control of the career fates of literators and poets. As a legend goes, the supernatural being of the Wen-qu Star always holds a pen in his hand; once touched by his pen, one would be able to become famous or successful. Thus, the tower was designed in a pen-like shape, and also called "Tower of Fame and Success".

余荫山房
Yu-yin Mountain House

位于番禺南村，又名余荫园，建于清同治六年，广东四大名园（其余三个是顺德清晖园、东莞可园、佛山梁园）之一，以小巧玲珑而著称，其布局巧妙，造出园中有园，景中有景，幽深广阔的境界，是岭南园林艺术的杰出代表。山房为邬燕天所建。邬及其长子、次子先后中举，特建园庆贺。上图为外景，中图分别是墙饰、匾额和园内景色，下图为室内结构。

Nestled in Nan-cun Town of Panyu District, alternatively called Yu-yin Park, and constructed in the 6th year of Tong-Zhi Emperor Reign of the ancient Qing Dynasty, and listed among the four most famous parks in Guangdong (the other 3 are: Qing-hui Park in Shunde, Ke's Park in Donggua, and Liang's Park in Foshan). Famed for its presentation of small and exquisite scenes, which are laid out in a dexterous manner. The House is seen as a typical representative of gardening arts of Guangdong Style. Originally constructed by Wu Yan-tan. As Wu Yan-tan, and his eldest son and second eldest son passed the imperial exams held in their province in succession, they constructed this House as a celebration. The upper picture shows the outer view of the House, the middle picture shows the adornments on walls, horizontal tablet with inscription and the scene inside the House respectively; whilst the lower picture shows the indoor structure.

文物景观

宝墨园
Bao-mo Park

位于番禺沙湾"包相府"侧,始建于清末。"包相府"建于清嘉庆年间,昔日包拯在端州为官,有"宝砚投江"清廉故事广为传颂,故乡人建宝墨园于府侧以志先哲盛德。园内有大量装饰性和欣赏性的陶塑、砖、灰、石、木雕,其中瓷塑浮雕《清明上河图》已被列入"大世界吉尼斯之最"。园内还展示有御笔、御砚、御墨和名人书画作品等。上图为园景远眺,中图分别为牌坊、浮雕及馆藏物品,下右图为"包相府"。

Nestled nearby the "Mansion of Prime Minister Bao Zheng", and initially built upon in the late times of the ancient Qing Dynasty. The "Mansion of Prime Minister Bao Zheng" was constructed during the Jia-qing Period of Qing Dynasty. At that time, Bao Zheng was serving as a governmental official at Duan-zhou, and became renowned for his outstanding probity and solid integrity. There came down a story "Precious Inkstone Thrown into the River" among the local folks, which spoke volumes for the solid determination of Bao Zheng in fighting against corruption. The countrymen of Bao Zheng later constructed the Bao-mo Park nearby to the mansion of Bao Zheng, in an aim to commemorate his great accomplishments. Inside the Bao-mo Park, there exist a host of decorative sculptures, bricks, stones and wooden artworks for appreciation; among others, the drawing titled "Yamato-e on a River on the Tomb-sweeping Day" (Chinese name: Qing-ming-shang-he-tu) which was a basso-relievo on porcelain and plastics has already been included in the Guinness World Record Book. In the park, there also exist royal pens, royal inkstones, royal ink and calligraphy & painting works of historical personages. The upper picture shows a far view of the park scene, the middle pictures show the memorial archway, basso-relievo and a collection of articles; the lower picture on the right shows the "Mansion of Prime Minister Bao Zheng".

文物景观

长洲镇
Chang-zhou Town

广州市第一批历史文化保护区之一，位于广州东南，在我国近代史上有极高的知名度，是广州乃至中国近代历史的缩影，如柯拜船坞就是中国第一代产业工人的诞生地；竹丝岗外国人公墓葬的是外国来华商人和政府官员等，黄埔军校则是广州作为革命策源地最重要的体现之一（详见近代史迹部分）。长洲岛现仍存有大量近现代史迹、清代炮台和古建筑、市集及古树名木。上图为柯拜船坞，中图为炮台，下中图为文塔，下右图为外国人墓。

Among the city's first group of protected areas for great historical and cultural values. Nestled in the southeastern part of Guangzhou, and enjoys a high reputation in China's modern history. Deemed as an epitome of the city, and even the whole country's, evolvements in modern times. For example, the Ke-bai Boatyard is where China' first very group of industrial workers emerged; the Burial Ground of Expatriates at Zhu-si-gang has housed the bodies of those foreign businessmen and governmental officials from abroad who passed away in Guangzhou; while Huang-pu Military Academy is one of the best-known symbols indicating the capacity of Guangzhou City as a revolution base (see details in the "Historic Sites in Modern Times" part). Chang-zhou Island today still hosts a hoard of latter-day and modern sites of historical value, emplacements and ancient architecture originated from the old Qing Dynasty, relics of ancient arcades, and ancient & precious trees. The upper picture shows the Ke-bai Boatyard, the middle picture shows the emplacement, the lower picture in the middle shows the Wen Tower, and the lower picture on the right shows the Burial Ground of Expatriates.

文物景观

沙面
Sha-mian

广州市第一批历史文化保护区之一，位于荔湾区南面。第二次鸦片战争中英法两国强租沙面为租界，开涌磊土，使沙面成为四面环水的岛，外国列强在中国的"国中之国"。沙面集中了列强所建的领事馆、银行、教堂、俱乐部、医院等建筑，反映了巴洛克、哥特、新古典主义及中西合璧等各种建筑风格，因此有万国建筑博物馆之誉。在市政府公布的首批、第二批古树名木中沙面有158株，占全市45.4%，因而沙面又有"绿色明珠"的美誉。图为各种建筑及古树名木。

Listed among the city's first group of protected areas for great historical and cultural values. Nestled in the southern part of Li-wan District. During the Opium War II, UK and France coercively rented Sha-mian as a concession of theirs, and launched civil engineering at full blast; as a result, Sha-mian turned out a small island surrounded by water at its four sides, and also a "small country of foreign powers" in China. Sha-mian has hosted a galaxy of consulate mansions, banks, churches, clubs, and hospitals built up by the then foreign powers, which feature an assortment of architectural styles, such as Baroque, Gothic, Neo-classical and West-meets-East, etc. Hence, Sha-mian was reputed as a host of architectural structures from across the world. On the list of the first and second batches of those ancient and precious trees entitled to protection that was promulgated by the city government, up to 158 are located at Sha-mian, constituting 45.4% in the total. Thus, Sha-mian earned a fame "green pearl". The picture illustrates assorted architectures and ancient & precious trees.

文物景观

十三行
The Thirteen Hongs

十三行指明末在广州设置的十三个主营外贸的官办牙行,在清代则是对外贸易商行的通称。明代的十三行主要散落在今人民南路两侧,从镇安路至仁济路,可考的有同文行、宝顺行、怡和行等。1861年后,官方已不能再垄断对外贸易,十三行逐渐破落,成为普通商行。上图、中图为描绘十三行的美术作品,下图为现今仍有大量小商行在经营的十三行路面。

Originally, the Thirteen Hongs refer to the 13 official-run business outlets that were established in Guangzhou in the late times of the Ming Dynasty, and specialized in foreign trade. Later in the Qing Dynasty, the Chinese pronunciation name, reading "Shi-San-Hang", of the Thirteen Hongs became a general name for those businesses that were engaged in foreign trade. Most of the originally thirteen hongs in the Ming Dynasty were located on the two sides of the present-day Renmin Road South, starting from Zhen-an Road and ending on Ren-ji Road. Among others, only Tong-wen Hong, Bao-shun Hong, and Yi- he Hong had their historical archives available for reference. After 1861, the then Chinese government was unable to monopolize the country's foreign trade any longer; as a result, the thirteen hongs saw their business revenues drop down progressively, and then turned to be ordinary businesses. The upper picture and the middle picture are the artistic works in description of the then scenarios going in the original 13 hongs; while the lower picture illustrates the scene on the road where the original 13 hongs were located, where there are still a lot of small businesses running nowadays.

文物景观

文物景观

上下九－第十甫
Shangxiajiu~Dishipu

广州市第一批历史文化保护区之一，位于荔湾区，是清末民初，继广州"十三行"后，至今仍然兴盛的又一个岭南著名的繁华商业中心。广州骑楼是适用本地气候、商业条件，具有浓郁地方和时代特点，并与西方文化相融合的传统建筑。上下九、第十甫路是目前广州规模最大，保存得较好，并且仍维持着商业繁华功能的骑楼建筑群。其周边有华林寺、荔湾博物馆和锦纶会馆等古迹，邻近还有经营玉器、酸枝家俱等商品专业街。下左图为平安大戏院，其余各图为街景。

Among the first group of protected areas for historical and cultural values in Guangzhou. Nestled in Li-wan District, it still remains a prosperous commercial hub. Initially it emerged between the late period of the Qing Dynasty and early 1912. The verandah-style house in Guangzhou has been an "East Meets West" fruit, and suitable for the local weather and conditions. Both the Shangxiajiu Road and the Dishipu Road have housed the largest group of best protected verandah-style houses, which still serve as business outlets, in today's China. In the vicinity of these houses, there lie other ancient relics such as the Hua-lin Temple, Li-wan Museum and Jin-lun Hall, etc., as well as other streets where a number of shops are specialized in dealing with jade products and Dalbergia cochinchinensis made furniture, etc. The picture on the left shows the Peace Theater, and the other pictures show snapshots on the streets.

邮政大楼
Post Office Mansion

位于沿江西路,新古典主义风格建筑,建成于1916年,曾先后作为广东邮务管理局、邮电部广州邮局和广州市邮政局办公楼,现为广州邮政博览馆。

Nestled in Yan-jiang Road West, a new-classical architectural structure. Built up in 1916, used as the office premises of Guangdong Province Postal Service Authority, Guangzhou Postal Service under the State Post & Communications Department and Guangzhou Municipal Postal Service Bureau in successions. Currently named Guangzhou Postal Service Museum.

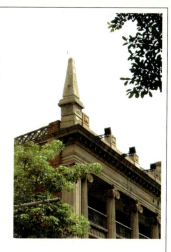

粤海关大楼
Guangdong Customs Office Mansion

位于沿江西路,俗称大钟楼,为欧洲新古典主义风格建筑。大楼反映了民国初期西方建筑风格与艺术对广州的影响。

Nestled in Yan-jiang Road, usually called the Big Bell Tower. Known as an architectural structure with a European neo-classical style. A living reflection of the influence exerted by the western architectural arts upon the city of Guangzhou in the early period of the Republic of China (1912-1949).

文物景观

荔湾博物馆
Li-wan Museum

位于龙津西路,为民初的中式庭园、西式建筑的富商别墅。1996年12月,在此处开办荔湾博物馆,为广东省第一个区级博物馆。馆内有风土民情、特色艺术、商业街市等内容的展示。实物包括了出土文物、西关大屋木雕、西关近代服饰、家具、日常用品等,还有不少珍贵的旧照片。各图均为馆内景致。

Nestled in Long-jin Road West, well-known for its fusion of the typical architectural style in the early period of the Republic of China (1912-1949) and the western style of architecture. Used to house a number of villas for rich businessmen. In December 1996, the museum emerged as a result of reconstruction work, and turned out the very first district-level museum in Guangdong province. Inside the museum, there is a galaxy of exhibits, which reveal the folk custom, characteristic arts and scenarios of commerce in the city. Objects in kind on display include excavated cultural relics, wood sculptures taken from those large residential houses of great cultural value in the western part of the city, latter-day clothes, furniture and everyday-use articles of traditional Cantonese style, as well as many photos. The pictures show different scenes in the museum.

文物景观

西关明清家居
Residences of traditional Ming and Qing Dynasties in the Western Downtown Area

西关大屋是明清时名门望族、富商巨贾和洋行买办阶层的豪宅，它除了必备的短脚吊扇门、趟栊、硬木大门"三件头"做得精工厚实外，其家居布置也是同样考究：屋内各种用途的厅堂、房间、天井和连廊里巧妙地布置了满洲窗、酸枝家具、落地摆钟、文房四宝、古玩陶瓷、乐器、盆景等，十分雍容华贵。各图均为西关大屋内外景致。

Large residential houses in the western downtown area of Guangzhou used to be occupied by those locally famed families, business tycoons and working personnel with foreign firms, and feature three major items: short-feet hung-type fan-shaped door, sliding lattice and hard-wood gate. Inside these houses, there exist an assortment of household adornments, which are put together to present a wholesome and chic atmosphere. The pictures show different views in these houses.

文物景观

耀华大街
Yao-hua Avenue

广州市第一批历史文化保护区之一,位于文昌北路,属清末民初开发的西关住宅区的一部分。街巷为东西走向,长约130米,宽5米,石板路完好,两侧40多栋西关传统民居鳞次栉比,基本上是石角大青砖和角门、趟栊、大门三件头样式,排列很整齐,整体视觉效果良好,有一定规模,类似这样整齐完好的成群连片的具有传统建筑特色的街巷在广州西关已属凤毛麟角。大街体现出当时中上层商人、手工业主和文化人士居住生活及相互亲和的社会文化风貌。各图均为街中景致。

Among the first group of protected areas for historical and cultural values in Guangzhou. Nestled in Wen-chang Road North. Constitutes a component part of the residential quarters in the western downtown area of Guangzhou, which was originally erected in the late period of Qing Dynasty and the early period of the Republic of China (1912-1949). The avenue extends from east to west, lasting a length of about 130 meters and being 5 meters wide. Covered by stone plates in good condition. On the two sides of the avenue, there exist over 40 residential houses, which are lined in order, and mostly constructed by use of big black bricks, corner gates, sliding lattices and hard-wooden gates, thus presenting a rather good visual effect. This is a precious block in today's western downtown area of Guangzhou where these traditional houses could be seen in one group. This avenue is a living manifestation of the then social and cultural scenes in which those upper-class businessmen, handicraftsmen, and writers. The pictures show different views on the avenue.

文物景观

新河浦
Xin-he-pu

广州市第一批历史文化保护区之一,位于东山区,是我市现存规模最大的中西结合的低层院落式民居群和历史街区。20世纪初,一批热心家乡建设的海外华侨买地置业,辟路建房,几十年间形成了大规模的住宅群。当时的住户多是华侨、侨眷及达官名人,由此带动了东山地区后来的繁荣发展。左上图为全景,其余各图为特色建筑。

Among the first group of protected areas for historical and cultural values in the city of Guangzhou. Nestled in Dong-shan District, known as a relatively big block hosting a number of "west-meets-east" low-rise residential houses of great historical value. In early 1920s, a galaxy of overseas Chinese who were ardently devoted to the construction cause in Guangzhou bought land sections and had roads built up and their own houses erected. Over dozens of years since then, the large-sized residential quarters came into being. At that time, most of the residents in here were returned overseas Chinese and their relatives, as well as some high officials and social personages, who contributed heavily to the prosperity and fast evolvement of Dong-shan District. The upper picture on the left shows the panorama, and the other pictures show the characteristic architectures.

文物景观

人民公园
The People's Park

位于吉祥路，广州历史最悠久的公园之一。原址从隋朝起至清末均为历代官署所在地，1917年孙中山倡议建成公园，称"第一公园"，1926年改名为"中央公园"，1966年改称"人民公园"至今，1998年市政府将其建成一个敞开式的绿化广场。上图为公园牌坊，右下图为清代白玉狮子，其余各图为现代雕塑及园内景致。

Nestled in Ji-xiang Road, one of the most historically renowned parks in Guangzhou. The original site of this park has been a residential place of state officials since Sui Dynasty and until the late period of Qing Dynasty. In 1917, Sun Yat-sen suggested building up a park in here, thus the later "No.1 Park". In 1926, the park was renamed to be the "Central Park", and has been renamed again in 1966 as the "People's Park" until now. In 1998, the city government dismantled the four enclosure walls of this park to make it open to the general public. The upper picture shows the archway of the park, the lower picture on the right shows the chauche lion that was sculpted in Qing Dynasty; the other pictures show the modern sculptures and internal views of the park.

文物景观

市府合署楼
He-Shu Mansion

位于府前路，为民国时期陈济棠主粤时的官署，由著名建筑师林克明设计。大楼前面为小广场与人民公园相连，楼两侧有百年古榕，绿盖成荫，一对高大石狮雄踞门前两侧草地，使这一宫殿式建筑更为庄重。1949年10月，广州解放，解放军入城仪式在这里举行。此后为市府办公大楼。各图为大楼景致。

Nestled in Fu-qian Road, used to be the office premises of Chen Ji-tang, a former mayor of the city of Guangzhou in the period of the Republic of China (1912-1949). Designed by a famed architect named Lin Ke-ming. In front of the mansion, there is a small square, which is connected to the People's Park. On the two sides of the mansion, there grow some a hundred-year-old banyan trees, accompanied by a pair of tall lion-shaped stone sculptures on the lawns. In October 1949, Guangzhou was liberated by the People's Liberation Army (PLA). The celebration ceremony for the PLA's entry into Guangzhou was held in here. After that, this mansion became the office premises of Guangzhou City Government. The pictures show the different views inside the mansion.

文物景观

文物景观

中山纪念堂
Zhong-shan Memorial Hall

位于东风中路,原址为清代抚标箭道,后为督练公所,辛亥革命后为督学署,1921 至 1922 年孙中山任非常大总统时,在此设立总统府。1922 年 6 月陈炯明叛变时炮击将之夷为平地。为纪念孙中山的伟大功绩,筹建了此纪念堂,由我国著名建筑师吕彦直设计,1931 年 10 月建成。上图为全景,其余各图为建筑室内外景致。

Nestled in Dong-feng Road Central, originally served as an archery court in Qing Dynasty, later used as a guild hall; then became a school after the Revolution of 1911. From 1921 to 1922 when Sun Yat-sen was acting as the extraordinary president of the then China, the presidential office was set up in here. In June 1922, that office was dismantled by bombardment when Chen Jiong-ming rose up. To commemorate the great accomplishments of Sun Yat-sen, this Memorial Hall was built up in October 1931, and designed by Lv Yan-zhi, a famous Chinese architect. The upper picture shows a panorama of the hall, while the other pictures show the interior and exterior scenes.

中山纪念碑
Zhong-shan Monument

位于越秀山。建于1929年，吕彦直设计，由花岗石砌成，碑高37米。外呈方形、尖顶。碑基上层四面围栏中共有26个羊石雕，象征羊城。

Nestled in the Yue-xiu Mount. Established in 1929, and designed by Lv Yan-zhi. Built up by use of granite, being 37 meters high. In a rectangular shape, with a steeple. There are a totally 26 sheep-shaped stone sculptures on the fencings on the four sides of the upper layer of the foundation, which symbolized the city of Guangzhou as a "city of rams".

孙中山读书治事处
Sun Yat-sen Office

位于越秀山。此处原址是孙中山和宋庆龄居住过粤秀楼。陈炯明发动叛乱时孙先生从这里脱险，碑上刻有总统府卫士与叛军浴血奋战的经过。

Nestled in the Yue-xiu Mount. Used to host the Yue-xiu Mansion, where Sun Yat-sen and his wife Song Qing-ling lived. When Chen Jiong-ming rose up, Sun fled from here. On the tablet there is a story which tells how the bodyguards of Sun Yat-sen fought against the rebels to protect Sun.

中山大学校门牌楼
Archway at the Gate of Zhong-shan University

位于五山路，上刻中山大学奠基民国24年（1935）及校长邹鲁和诸董事的姓名。牌楼横额原镌刻"国立中山大学"，建国后改书"为人民服务"。

Nestled in Wu-shan Road, bearing carved characters which read "the university was set up in 1935" and the names of the then Chancellor Zou Lu and those trustees. The horizontal tablet used to bear the Chinese characters of the university's name, which were later replaced by a phrase meaning "serve the people".

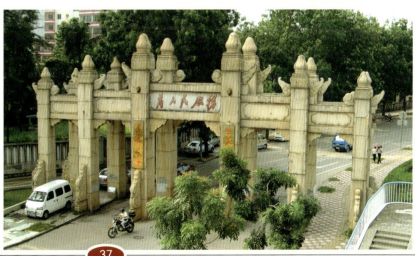

华侨新村
Returned Overseas Chinese New Village

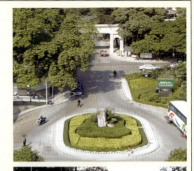

广州市第一批历史文化保护区之一，位于环市东路。建国后广州市委、市政府非常重视侨务工作，新村由政府拨款和归侨集资于1965年建成。总建筑面积近十二万平方米，这在当时国民经济困难的情况下是非常不易的，同时也是全国大城市中唯一的最大型华侨居住区。其建筑依地形布局，2—3层低密度。

Among the first group of protected areas for historical and cultural values in Guangzhou City. Nestled in Huan-shi Road East. After 1949, the then City Government of Guangzhou and the Chinese Communist Party in the City attached great importance to the relationships with returned overseas Chinese. The village was built up in 1965, by use of financial appropriation by the city government and money pooled together by certain returned overseas Chinese. The total building area reaches up to 120,000 square meters. This is a great accomplishment, considering the then financial strengths of the city government; and has also been the exclusive residential quarters, special for hosting returned overseas Chinese, in the entire country. Most of the houses in this village are 2 or 3 storeyed.

说明：左上图为全景，左中图为学校，右上图为新村入口，其余各图为特色建筑和街景。

Annotations: the upper picture on the left shows the panorama of the village, the middle picture on the left shows the school, the upper picture on the right shows the entrance to the village; and the other pictures show the snapshots of characteristic buildings and streets inside the village.

文物景观

古树名木
Ancient and Precious Trees

古树名木是活的历史，蕴涵着丰富的信息，具有重要的历史价值、纪念意义以及重要的科研价值。历史悠久的广州有大量珍贵的古树名木，左上、右下图分别为中山纪念堂后面近320年树龄的木棉树和海幢公园近400年树龄的鹰爪兰树；右上图为孙中山在潘达微墓旁手植的松树。

Ancient and precious trees are the living witnesses of history, and of great historical, memorial and scientific research values. As a time-honored city, Guangzhou has housed a huge number of precious and ancient trees. The upper picture on the left and lower picture on the right respectively show an almost-320-year-old ceiba tree behind the Zhong-shan Memorial Hall, and a nearly-400-year-old Eagle-claw-orchid tree in the Hai-zhuang Park; the upper picture on the right shows the pine tree which was planted by Sun Yat-sen in person, near the tomb of Pan Da-wei.

文物景观

光孝寺
Guang-xiao Temple

位于光孝路,是岭南地区年代古老、规模最大的一座佛教名刹。民谚说:"未有羊城,先有光孝。"寺址原是西汉初年南越王赵佗的玄孙赵德建故宅。东晋时称五园寺,唐代称乾明法性寺,五代南汉时称乾亨寺,北宋时称万寿禅寺,南宋时称报恩广孝寺,明时称光孝寺。"光孝菩提"是宋羊城八景之一。上图为六祖瘗发塔,其余各图为寺内景致及牌匾。

Nestled in Guang-xiao Road, known as an ancient, and the largest-sized of its type, is the Buddhist temple in the Ling-nan Region (i.e. the south of the Five Ridges, the area covering Guangdong and Guangxi provinces). As an old Chinese saying goes, "Guang-xiao Temple emerged before the city of Guangzhou came into being". The site of the temple used to host the residence of Zhao Jian-de, the great-great-grandson of Zhao Tuo, the Nan-yue King in the early period of Western Han Dynasty. In the Eastern Jin Dynasty, it was called "Wu-Yuan Temple", and later renamed as "Qian-ming-fa-xing Temple" in Tang Dynasty. In the South Han Dynasty of the Five Dynasties Times, it was called "Qian Heng Temple". In the Northern Song Dynasty, it was called Wan Shou Chan Temple; in the Southern Song Dynast, it was called Bao En Guang Xiao Temple; and in the Ming Dynasty, it was named Guang Xiao Temple. The scene "Banyan Tree in Guang Xiao Temple is listed among the eight major scenic attractions it the city of Guangzhou. The upper picture shows the Liu-zu-yi-fa Tower, and the other pictures show the scenes in the temple and the tablet.

宗教遗存

南海神庙
South Sea Mortuary Temple

位于黄埔庙头村,又称菠萝庙,是我国古代对外贸易的一处重要史迹。它创建于隋朝开皇年间,已有1400多年的历史,为我国古代四大海神庙中唯一留存的一座。南海神庙是古代祭海的场所。1992年2月联合国教科文组织证实这里是中国古代"海上丝绸之路"的发源地。神庙为历史上的羊城八景之一。上图为康熙亲书的"万里波澄"碑,右下图为为"番鬼望波罗"像,其余各图为神庙景致。

Nestled in Miao-tou Village in Huang-pu District, alternatively called "Pineapple Temple". Known as an important witness of the country's foreign trade in ancient times. Initially constructed in the Kai Huang Reign of Sui Dynasty, is over 1,400 years old so far. The exclusive temple that still exists nowadays, is among the four major ancient Sea-God Temples in China. Used by the general public to offer sacrifice to the Sea God. In February 1992, UNESCO proved that this temple was the very starting point of the "Marine Silk Road" of China. The temple has been considered as one of the city's eight major scenic attractions, in history. The upper picture shows the inscription written by Kang Xi Emperor in person, while the lower picture on the right shows a figure of God, the other pictures show the scenes elsewhere in the temple.

宗教遗存

华林寺
Hua-lin Temple

位于长寿西路,是广州别具意义的佛教寺院。在南朝梁普通年间,印度高僧菩提达摩航海西来,于今的上、下九路附近登岸,结草为庵,开中国佛教禅宗之源。后人称此地为西来初地,称庵为西来庵。历隋、唐、宋、元、明诸朝代,传灯不息。清初宗符禅师募集资金建大雄宝殿,道光二十九年始建五百罗汉堂。下左图为达摩塑像,下右图为罗汉堂。

Nestled in Chang-shou Road West, known as a characteristic Buddhist temple of special significance in Guangzhou. During the Liang-pu-tong Reign of the Southern Dynasty in ancient times, a senior monk sailed from India to arrive at some place near today's Shangxiajiu of Guangzhou, and built up a grass hut, thus starting to disseminate Buddhism throughout China. Later, people called this place as Xi-lai Hut. This hut remained here throughout Sui, Tang, Song, Yuan, and Ming Dynasties. In the earth period of Qing Dynasty, a Buddhist monk called Zong Fu raised funds to build up a Da-Xiong Hall. In the 29th year of Dao-guang Emperor's Reign, the 500-Arhat Hall was constructed. The lower picture on the left shows the figure of that Indian monk; whilst the lower picture on the right shows the Arhat Hall.

宗教遗存

六榕寺
Six-Banyan-Tree Temple

位于六榕路,广州四大佛教丛林之一,始建于梁大同三年,距今1400多年。元符三年苏东坡曾来寺游览,见寺内有老榕六株,欣然题书"六榕"二字,后人遂称为六榕寺。该寺为迎"舍利"而建"宝庄严寺舍利塔",俗称花塔。塔利铸 工精巧,上密布1023尊小佛像,连同构件重逾5吨,庄严瑰丽,直指苍穹。上左图为花塔全貌,其余各图为寺内景致。

Nestled in the Six-Banyan-Tree Road, one of the four major Buddhist bases in Guangzhou. Initially built in the 3rd year of Liang Da-tong Reign, thus being over 1,400 years old so far. In the 3rd year of Yuan-fu Regin, Su Dong-po (a great writer in the ancient history of China) once visited the temple, and saw the six old banyan trees; he then joyfully wrote down two Chinese characters "Liu Rong" (which means six banyan trees) as an inscription. Since that, the temple was called "Six-Banyan Tree Temple". A pagoda was later established and called by the multitude as "Colored Tower", featuring 1,023 small Buddhist figures of exquisite craftsmanship; together with other component parts, the pagoda weighs nearly 5 tons heavy. The upper picture on the left shows the panorama of the Colored Tower, the other pictures show the scenes in he temple.

宗教遗存

大佛寺
Great Buddha Temple

位于惠福路,为广府五大丛林之一。其前身为南汉二十八寺中之新藏寺,明代扩建为龙藏寺,康熙年间,尚可喜自捐王体重建,布局及制式悉仿京师官庙,为北方风格。寺中的3尊大佛为岭南之冠,故名大佛寺。道光年间,林则徐禁烟时在此设立了"收缴烟土烟枪总局";1926年,周恩来在此开办培训班,培养了50多名高级政治干部,蒋介石也为学员讲话。上图为佛寺大门,下右图为寺中大佛。

Nestled in Hui-fu Road. Formerly known as Xin-zang Temple; later expanded and renamed as Long Cang Temple in Ming Dynasty. In the Kang Xi Emperor Reign, Shang Ke-xi had this temple rebuilt according to a layout design similar to that employed by those state-established temples in the capital city, featuring a northern style of architecture. The 3 Buddha figures are the largest ones of their kind, thus the temple was called Great Buddha Temple. During the Dao Guang Emperor Reign, Lin Ze-xu set up an "Opium Confiscation Bureau General" in here. In 1926, Zhou En-lai launched a training school, where over 50 senior political cadres were trained up, and Chiang Kai-shek delivered speeches to the trainees, too. The upper picture shows the main gate to the temple, and the lower picture on the right shows the Great Buddha figure in the temple.

海幢寺
Hai Zhuang Temple

位于南华中路,是清代广州佛教四大丛林之一。寺处相传为南汉千秋寺所在地。明朝末年,僧人光牟在此地挂上"海幢"门匾,取滨海佛寺之意。清初巡抚刘某捐资正式建成山门。清嘉庆年间寺院特别辟为夷人游览区,专门接待外国游客。上图为雄伟的藏经阁,其余各图为寺内景致。

Nestled in Nan-hua Road Central, said to be called Qian Qiu Temple in the Southern Han Dynasty. In the late period of Ming Dynasty, a monk called Guang Mou put up a door tablet with two Chinese characters reading as "Hai Zhuang", which meant the host of Buddha on the seaside. In the early period of Qing Dynasty, an imperial inspector whose surname was Liu donated money to build up a gate to the hill. In the Jia Qing Emperor Reign of Qing Dynasty, the temple was opened only to foreign tourists. The upper picture shows the splendid Scripture Tower, and the other pictures show the scenes inside the temple.

宗教遗存

三元宫
San-yuan Palace

位于越秀山南麓，前身是越岗院，建于大兴二年，为南海太守鲍靓的修行成道之所。明万历年间改名三元宫。其山门高出地面40余级石阶，石门旁镶石刻对联"三元古观，百粤名山"。主殿三元殿与钟楼和拜廊连成一片，建筑风格十分独特。三元宫是广州流行的上元诞、中元诞、下元诞的活动地。上图为三元宫大门，其余各图为宫中景致。

Nestled at the southern foot of Yue-xiu Mount, used to be called Yue-gang Court, where Bao Liang, a procurator at Nan-hai cultivated himself according to the religious doctrine. Initially built up in the 2nd year of Da Xing Times. In the Wan-li Reign of Ming Dynasty, renamed as San-yuan Palace. The gate of the palace is over 40 stone stairs higher than the ground level, and there is a couplet sculpted on the stone gate. The main hall, San-yuan Hall, and the Bell Tower, and the Worship Corridor are all connected with one another, presenting a rather unique architectural style. The upper picture shows the main gate, and the other pictures show the interior scenes of the palace.

宗教遗存

五仙观
Five-Immortal Temple

位于惠福西路,南汉唐时为府尹祭祀的谷神祠、建于药洲旁,又称奉真观。明洪武十年迁至坡山处。相传周夷王时,有五位仙人骑着口含谷穗的五头羊飞临广州,把谷穗赠给广州人,祝愿广州永无饥荒。故广州又叫羊城、穗城。人们为了纪念五位仙人,建造此观,塑五仙骑羊像,奉祀观内。下左图为"仙人拇迹",其余各图为观中景致。

Nestled in Hui-fu Road West, used to be called "God of Grain" temple in ancient times. Built up near the Yao Zhou, and alternatively called Feng Zhen Temple. Relocated to a hillside in the 10th year of Hong Wu Emperor Reign of Ming Dynasty. As a legend goes, in the time of Zhou Yi King Reign, five immortals each rode a ram with a wheat ear in its mouth to fly to Guangzhou, and gave these wheat ears to residents in Guangzhou, and wished people in Guangzhou would never suffer hunger. Thus, Guangzhou is also called a city of rams/wheat ears. To memorize these five immortals, people have constructed this temple, and sculpted a figure featuring "5 immortals each riding on a ram". The lower picture on the left shows the "print of immortal's thumb", and the other pictures show the scenes in the temple.

宗教遗存

仁威庙
Ren Wei Temple

位于荔湾湖东北,始建于1052年,为供祀真武帝君的庙宇。真武帝即玄武帝,"玄"者黑也,故又称"黑帝",道教尊之为北方之神。庙中建筑雕饰集丹青、木刻、砖雕、灰雕等各种艺术于一体,生动传神,集中了岭南古建筑艺术的精华,曾被誉为"桂殿兰宫"。晚清时该庙宇成为民间集会结社之所。上图为庙宇全景,其余各图为庙中景致。

Nestled to the northeast to the Li-wan Lake, initially erected in 1052 to offer sacrifice to Zhen-wu Emperor (i.e. Xuan-wu King, the God of China's North). The architecture in here makes a fusion of painting, wood sculpting, brick sculpting and ash shaping arts, presenting a vivid manifestation of the assorted artistic genres in Guangdong and Guangxi provinces. In the late period of the Qing Dynasty, this temple hosted a number of folk get-togethers. The upper picture shows the panorama of the temple, and the other pictures show different scenes in the temple.

宗教遗存

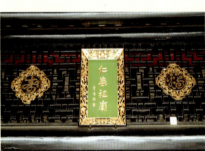

宗教遗存

白云仙馆
White Clouds Fairy Hall

位于麓湖公园，建于清嘉庆十七年，原名"云泉仙馆"。山门石柱刻有楹联"香火千年祖庭瞻仰，白云四面仙客栖迟"。殿柱有楹联"白云初晴幽鸟相逐 流水今日明月前身"，题字落款为全国政协副主席赵朴初。仙馆初为广州文人墨客雅集之地。后来供奉八仙之一的吕洞宾，有道士主持管理。上左图为仙馆大门，其余各图为仙馆内外景致。

Nestled in the Li-hu Park, initially erected in the 17th year of Jia-qing Emperor Reign of Qing Dynasty. Originally called "Cloud and Fairy Hall". There are couplets on the tablets at the entrance to the Hall and on the columns inside the Hall, as well as an inscription by Zhao Pu-chu, former Vice Chairman with the Chinese People's Political Consultative Conference. At the beginning of its establishment, the Hall was a rendezvous for the then writers and poets in Guangzhou. Later, the Hall was used to offer sacrifice to Lv Dong-bin, one of the eight immortals in a folk legend, and administered by some Taoist. The upper picture shows the main gate to the Hall, and the other pictures show different scenes in the Hall.

纯阳观
Chun-yang Hall

位于新港西路，建于清道光四年，主持者是担任观主的广州道士李明彻。李是著名道士，又是一个天文学家，因此观中除修筑殿堂外，还修筑了一个可供观测星象的朝斗台。现山门石额"纯阳观"三个篆体字出自当年曾为两广总督的大学士阮元手笔。纯阳殿供祀的是"纯阳子"，八仙之一的吕洞宾。上图为纯阳宫大门，其余各图为宫内外景致。

Nestled in Xin-gang Road West, initially erected in the 4th year of Dao-guang Emperor Reign of Qing Dynasty, and hosted by Li Ming-che, a Taoist in Guangzhou. Li was a well-known Taoist, and also an astronomer. Therefore, in addition to halls, a platform where visitors could observe the stars in the sky was erected. The three Chinese characters "Chun Yang Guan" on the stone tablet at the gate were written by Ruan Yuan, a great scholar at that time. The Hall was established to offer sacrifice to Chun Yang Zi, namely, Lv Dong-bin, one of the eight immortals in a folk legend. The upper picture shows the main gate, and the other picture show different scenes in the Hall.

宗教遗存

黄大仙祠
Huang-da-xian Ancestral Temple

位于芳村花地,相传建于清咸丰六至八年,清光绪三十年重修后成为一座蔚为壮观的儒、释、道三教合一的庙宇,为民赠医施药,曾名闻广东,求神拜佛者众。黄大仙是何方神圣历来说法不一,一说是浙江的黄初平,另一说是广东的黄野人。仙祠主殿有重2吨多的青铜黄大仙像;偏殿除了设吕祖等人像外,还设置了相貌奇特的斗姥像。中右图为仙祠大门,其余各图为仙祠内外景致。

Nestled in Hua-di of Fang-cun District, said be erected between the 6th year to the 8th year of Xian-feng Emperor Reign of Qing Dynasty. Reconstructed in the 30th year of Guang-xu Emperor of Qing Dynasty and thus became a splendid temple that makes a fusion of Confucianism, Buddhism and Taoism. The monks in the temple were highly regarded for their free provision of medical advice and even drugs to the multitude in need of medical service. It still remains uncertain how the Huang-Da-Xian (angel immortal) was originated; some said the prototype was Huang Chu-ping in Zhejiang province; others said the prototype was Huang Ye-ren in Guangdong Province. In the main hall of the Fairly Temple, there lies a bronze figure of Huang Da-xian that weighs in at over 2 tons; in the side hall, there also exists a Dou-lao Figure with a unique face look, in addition to the images of Lv Zu, etc. The middle picture on the right shows the main gate, while the other pictures show the interior and exterior scenes.

宗教遗存

圣心大教堂
Sacred Heart Cathedral

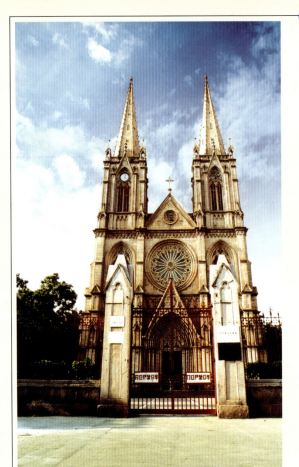

著名的天主教堂，位于一德路，是我国最大的一座双尖塔哥特式石结构建筑物。清同治二年兴建，因主要用花岗石砌筑而成，故又称"石室"。教堂前半部是两座巍峨高耸的尖顶石塔，寓意是向天升华，皈依上帝。后半部是大礼堂，门窗镶嵌有红、黄、蓝、绿各种图案的套色玻璃，光线柔和，气氛肃穆。左上图为教堂全貌，其余各图为教堂内外景致。

A renowned Catholic church, nestled in Yi-De Road, known as the largest dual-steepled Gothic stone structure in China. Erected in the 2nd year of Tong-Zhi Emperor Reign of Qing Dynasty. Also called a "Stone Chamber", for it was constructed chiefly in granite. The front half of the church is characterized by two steepled stone towers, which augur loyalty to the God. The rear half of the church is covered by a great hall, whose doors and windows are embedded with colored glasses in red, yellow, blue and green, creating a soft but solemn lighting atmosphere. The upper picture on the left shows the panorama of the church, whilst the other pictures show the interior and exterior scenes of the church.

宗教遗存

东山堂
Dong-shan Hall

位于寺贝通津，是著名的基督教教堂。其建筑设计摈弃古典式的繁纹缛饰，代之以简洁明快的线条，殿廊壁柱等均不事雕饰。教堂的建筑规模较小，装饰也较朴素，这恐怕与当年教会的势力或财力不大有关。教堂的兴建时间是上世纪的20年代还是30年代，众说不一。教堂内设广州目前唯一的一所宗教学院。上图为东山堂全貌，下右图为大门。
Nestled in Si-bei-tong-jin, known as a famed Christian church. Its architectural style is streamlined, simple but impressive, instead of being classical and complicated. The corridors, walls and columns bear no carving adornments. The church covers a relatively small area and is decorated in a simple fashion, which might be a result of the limited strength or financial power of the then church. It still remains unknown exactly when the church was erected, in 1920s or 1930s. Inside the church, there exists the exclusive religious college in today's Guangzhou. The upper picture shows the panorama of Dong-shan Hall, and the middle picture on the right shows its main gate.

宗教遗存

怀圣寺
Huai-sheng Temple

位于光塔路，是伊斯兰教传入中国最早兴建的清真寺，又称光塔寺、怀圣光塔寺，始建于唐代。寺内有看月楼，具有中国建筑风格。礼拜殿坐西朝东，按伊斯兰教规，教徒礼拜时，面向圣地麦加。怀圣寺是中国与伊斯兰教国家人民友好往来的历史见证，是研究中国海外交通史以及伊斯兰教的重要古迹。上图为光塔外景，中图为匾额。

Nestled in the Guang-Ta Road, known as the earliest mosque emerging in China after Islam was ushered into China. Alternatively called Guang-Ta Temple, or Saint Guang-Ta Temple. Initially established in the ancient Tang Dynasty. Inside the temple, there is a Moon Viewing Tower, which is designed in traditional Chinese architectural style. The divine service hall faces eastward. According to the Islamic canon, followers of Islam shall face the Holy Land of Mecca during the course of divine service. The Huai-sheng Temple is a witness of the friendly exchanges between the Chinese people and their counterparts in those Islamic countries, and also an important place of great values for research into the origin of Islam in China and the history of China's communications with the rest of the world. The upper picture shows the exterior view of the Guang-Ta Tower, and the middle picture shows the horizontal tablet with an inscription.

清真先贤古墓
Mausoleum of Ancient Islamic Sage

位于解放北路。元代以来，中国境内的穆斯林被称为"回回"，因而这里亦叫回回坟。明清中国学者称伊斯兰教义"至清至真"，称该教为"清真教"。据墓碑介绍，这些先贤奉穆罕默德的遣使来华传教，在一次礼拜时，大家遵教规用心专一，因此，当强盗挥舞屠刀时，他们个个仍纹丝不动，及至全被杀尽。上图为合葬墓，其余各图为墓园内外景致。

Nestled in the Jie-fang Road North. Since Yuan Dynasty, the Muslims in China have been called "Hui-hui people". Hence, this place was alternatively called the tomb of Hui-hui. Chinese scholars who are engaged in research of the country's histories in Ming and Qing Dynasties said that the canon of Islam is "the purest and simplest one"; thus Islam is also called "Religion of Purity and Simplicity" According to the introductory words on the gravestone, these diplomatic envoys dispatched by the sage Mahomet came to China to do missionary work. Once when they were fully devoted to divine service, invaders broke in and brandished butcher knives; but they stayed put in their seats, until they were finally killed. The upper picture shows the tomb of these pilgrims, and the other pictures show the exterior view of the tomb yard.

宗教遗存

花都盘古王庙
Pan-gu King Temple at Hua-du Town

位于花都狮岭，倚盘古王山而建，建于清嘉庆十四年，是一座琉璃瓦面的殿堂式建筑物。殿堂正中端坐着盘古王神像。有四个阶梯式的大拜坛，可容纳千人朝拜。盘古王庙历年香火不绝，逢农历八月十二日盘古王诞，珠三角许多民众擂鼓舞狮，前来庆贺。山上有泉称为"圣水"，朝拜者皆取水祈愿保平安。上图为盘古王庙全貌，中右图为盘古王塑像，其余各图为庙内外景致。

Nestled in the Lion Hill of Hua-du Town, nearby the Pan-gu King Mount. Initially erected in the 14th year of Jia-qing Emperor Reign of Qing Dynasty. A hall-style architectural structure decorated with glass tiles. In the middle of the hall of this temple, there exists a figure of the legendary Pan-gu King. There are four ladder-shaped big altars, on which up to 1,000 pilgrims could be hosted. The incense is burnt in the temple throughout the year. On August 12 of each year in the Chinese lunar calendar, an event was held to celebrate the birth of Pan-gu King. On that day, many people hailing from all across the Pearl River Delta region beat drums and put up dragon dances as celebrations. On the mount by the temple, there is a spring called "Source of Saint Water", from which pilgrims take water in a wish to ask for good luck for themselves. The upper picture shows a bird's view of the temple, the picture on the right shows the sculpture of the Pan-gu King, and the other pictures show the scenes inside and outside the temple.

宗教遗存

番禺学宫
Panyu Study House

位于中山四路,明清时赫赫有名的岭南"第一学府",建于明洪武三年,是明清时期番禺县的县学和祭祀孔子的场所。学宫昔日规模宏大,"广3路,深5进"。现存的中路建筑包括棂星门、拱桥、大成门、大成殿、崇圣殿等。学宫在第一次国内革命战争时期曾作为培养农民运动干部的讲习所。上图为明伦堂外貌,中左图为学宫匾额。

Nestled in the Zhong-shan No. 4 Road, well-known as the "No.1 Study House" in Ling-nan Area (i.e. the south of the Five Ridges, the area covering Guangdong and Guangxi provinces). Initially set up in the 3rd year of Hong-wu's Reign of the Ming Dynasty. Used to be the school of Panyu County in the Ming and Qing Dynasties and the place to offer sacrifice to Confucius. The House used to cover a large area. The House of today is composed of Ling-Xing Gate, an arch bridge, Da-cheng Gate, Da-cheng Hall, and Chong-sheng Hall, etc. During the first domestic revolutionary war period, this House was used as the premises for training up those cadres for playing active roles in the peasants' revolutionary campaign. The upper picture shows the exterior view of the Ming-lun Hall, and the middle picture on the left shows the horizontal tablet with an inscription.

书院场馆

陈氏书院
Chen's Academy

位于中山七路，俗称为陈家祠，现是广东民间工艺博物馆所在地，清光绪十六年兴建，是当时广东72县陈姓合族宗祠。始建时用作广东各县陈氏子弟来省应科举时学习及住宿场所，也是祭祀祖宗的宗祠。主体建筑规模宏大，厅堂轩昂，庭院幽雅，全院的门、窗、屏、墙、栏、梁架、屋脊等处处均配上精美的各式木雕、石雕、砖雕、灰塑、陶塑、铜铁铸等艺术品。雕刻中还有历代历史故事和民间传说，被赞誉为"木刻钢刀雕就的中国历史故事长廊"。上图为书院外貌，其余各图为院内景致。

Nestled in Zhong-shan No.7 Road, normally called Chen's Clan Temple. Currently serves as the site of Guangdong Folk Arts Museum. Initially erected in the 16th year of Guang-xu Emperor's Reign of Qing Dynasty. Used to be the temple of all those people sharing a "Chen" surname in 72 counties in the then Guangdong province. When initially established, it was used as a study and accommodation place for those students sharing a "Chen" surname from different counties in Guangdong province, and also as a place where sacrifice was offered to the ancestors. The principal architectural structure looks in a splendid and tasteful fashion. Exquisite wood sculptures are seen here and there, on all the doors, windows, screens, guardrails and beams as well as ridges of houses, accompanied by fine stone/brick/ceramic/copper/iron sculptures and ash shaped work-pieces. These sculptures also tell true-to-life stories and folk legends, thus reputed as the "living exhibition of China's history". The upper picture shows the exterior view of the academy, and the other pictures show the scenes inside.

书院场馆

大小马站——流水井
Da-xiao-ma-zhan~~Liu-shui-jing

广州市第一批历史文化保护区之一,位于北京路,现存清代中、晚期的古书院12间,是我市旧城区内唯一尚存成群成片古书院的历史地段。它反映了广州历史上浓厚的文化教育风气,是广州作为岭南文化教育中心的见证。古书院以宗 族形式兴建,多兼用宗族祠堂,主要为本乡(族)学子赴考提供补习、食宿场所。大、小马站——流水井仍保持明清代的街巷格局;文阁楼、奎文楼和流水井巷内古井仍存;周边有三朝古城墙、六脉渠、药洲等文物古迹和遗址。图为三家典型的书院及古井。

Among the first group of protected areas for historical and cultural values in the city of Guangzhou. Nestled in Beijing Road. There still exist 12 ancient houses, constructed in the style of the middle and late periods of the Qing Dynasty. This is considered as the exclusive block of ancient study houses in the old city area of today's Guangzhou. It reveals a reminder of the wholesome cultural and educational scene in the city of Guangzhou in ancient times, and has witnessed the educational development in the local region. These study houses were also used as temples to offer sacrifice, and to host those students of the same clan for the good of their study and accommodation. Nowadays, this block still preserves the ancient lane and alley layout originated in Ming and Qing Dynasties. Your eyes will savor the Wen-ge Tower, Kui-wen Tower and the ancient well in the Liu-shui-jing Lane. In the vicinity, there are also other cultural relics, such as the ancient city wall of the Three Dynasties, Six-pulse Canal, and Ya-zhou, etc. The picture shows three typical study houses and the ancient well.

书院场馆

横沙街
Heng-sha Street

广州市第一批历史文化保护区之一,位于大沙镇,又称书香街,是一条由众多具有岭南特色的建筑物组成的古色古香的街道。书香街始建于元代,重修于清代道光、咸丰、光绪各年代。街道共有85间祠堂或古书塾式的建筑,是我市现存古书院最集中、格局最完整的一条历史街区。上图为横沙街牌坊,其余各图为家塾牌匾及室内摆设。

Among the first group of protected areas for historical and cultural values in the city of Guangzhou. Nestled in Da-sha Town, alternatively called Shu-xiang Street. Known for its housing of a galaxy of Ling-nan styled architectural structures. Initially constructed in Yuan Dynasty, and reconstructed in the Dao Guang/Xian Feng/Guang Xu Emperors' Reigns discretely of Qing Dynasty. The street hosts in total 85 temples and study houses, considered as the very block of best-protected ancient study houses in today's China. The upper picture shows the archway in Heng-sha Street, and the other pictures show the tablets and interior adornments.

书院场馆

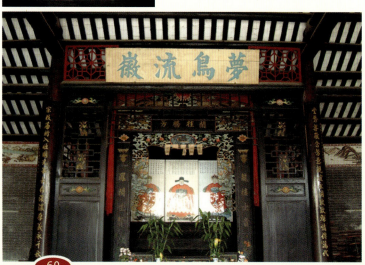

广雅书院
Guang-Ya Academy

位于西村,即今广雅中学前身,为清代的两广总督张之洞创立。他创办广雅书院的目的是培养"廉洁厚重"之士,以"效用国家"、"仪型乡里"。广者,大也,博也;雅者,正也,不俗也。要培养出学识广博而又品行雅正的人才。此外,"广"字也兼有广东、广州含义。张在创办广雅书院的同期,还在南园创办了广雅书局。下图为书院全貌,其余各图为院内外景致。

Nestled in Xi-cun Village, the prototype of today's Guang-ya High School, initially established by Zhang Zhi-dong, the governor of Guangdong and Guangxi provinces in former times. Zhang set up Guangz-ya Academy in an aim to cultivate human talents of probity and integrity, loyalty to the country and good manners. In addition to the establishment of Guang-ya Academy, Zhang also set up a Guang-ya Publishing House in the Southern Park. The lower picture shows the panorama of the Guang-ya Academy, and the other pictures show different scenes of the academy.

书院场馆

小蓬仙馆
Xiao-peng-xian Hall

原址在花地街上市新隆沙东，2002年搬迁重建于醉观公园，康有为的祖父建于清道光年间，为水磨青砖的三进建筑，坐北向南，有大殿、精舍，殿后还有小花园，亭台山石等，但可惜大部分建筑现已不存。以"仙馆"为名乃是当时的一种风气，以示高雅脱俗。清同治年间幼的康有为曾在此读书。上图为仙馆外貌，其余各图为仙馆内外景致。

Formerly located at Shang-shi Xin-long Sha-dong in Hua-di Street, relocated to Zui-guan Park as a result of reconstruction work in 2002. Initially constructed by the grandfather of Kang You-wei in the Dao-guang Emperor Regin of Qing Dynasty. Laid out in a triple structure, constructed by use of black bricks. Faces southwards, composed of a main hall, small houses, a little garden, pavilion, platform and artificial hill, etc. (unfortunately most of which have been destroyed). Kang You-wei once studied in here when he was a little boy, during the Tong-zhi Emperor Reign of Qing Dynasty. The upper picture shows the exterior look of the hall, and the other pictures show the exterior and interior scenes of the Hall.

书院场馆

万木草堂
Wan-mu-cao Hall

位于中山四路，原为邱氏书室。1891年康有为在此创办草堂讲学，宣传维新思想，培养变法维新骨干。学生如梁启超等都是戊戌变法的重要人物。图为草堂遗址现貌。

Nestled in Zhong-shan No.4 Road, used to be the study house of Qiu's. In 1891, Kang You-wei gave speeches in here to disseminate the thoughts of reform and to train up backbone talents to initialize the reform. His students, such as Liang Qi-chao, turned out important contributors to the Wu-xu Reform Campaign. The picture shows the current look of the relics of the Hall.

书院场馆

书院遗存
Relics of Study Houses

广州素以人文鼎盛而著称，曾在明清时代遍布广州的书院祠堂就是其中一个很好的佐证。图为部分书院的匾额、牌坊和遗址标志。

Guangzhou has been renowned for her rich cultural and humanistic scenarios over a long history. The relics of those study houses that once pervaded the city of Guangzhou in ancient times speak volumes for the wholesome educational scene in Guangzhou. The picture shows the horizontal tablets, archways and symbols of some of these study houses.

广东省立中山图书馆
Zhong-shan Library of Guangdong Province

位于文明路,创建于1912年,是我国大型综合性公共图书馆之一;典藏丰富,在海内外闻名遐迩,接待读者人次、流通图书册次皆位于全国前列;在图书采选、编目和读者服务等领域基本实现了计算机管理,为我国第一个实用化的省级数字图书馆。

Nestled in Wen-ming Road, initially set up in 1912, considered as one of the large-sized public libraries in China. It houses a great number of collected books, and enjoys a solid reputation both at home and abroad. The library has come out top, when compared to other libraries in the country, in terms of the number of patrons and the quantity of books in circulation. So far, the library has already employed computerized management practices in terms of book locating and selecting, catalogue-compiling and provision of service to readers, on the whole, thus having become the very first provincial-level digitalized library in China.

书院场馆

广州图书馆
Guangzhou Library

位于中山四路,1982年正式开馆,是一座大型、综合性的公共图书馆,以港澳台文献、广州地方文献、音像资料、电子信息资源丰富为特色;与法国里昂、日本福冈等图书馆进行图书交换和馆员交流;与美国、德国、新西兰有关图书馆 互赠图书,增进国际交流。

Nestled in Zhong-shan No.4 Road, opened officially to the public in 1982. Known as a large-sized and comprehensive public library. Mainly houses local literatures and others from HK, Macao and Taiwan, audio-video materials and electronic information resources. The library has been exchanging books and librarians with its counterparts in Lyons of France and Fukouka of Japan, and those libraries in USA, Germany and New Zealand, thus to promote the international exchanges.

广东省博物馆
Guangdong Provincial Museum

位于文明路,1959年建成南陈列馆并正式对外开放,是地志性的综合省级博物馆。它通过征集、收藏文物、标本,进行科学研究和举办具有地方特色的陈列展览,《馆藏陶瓷精品展览》有新石器时代至明清的全国各地精美陶瓷,广东石湾陶瓷、广彩等。上图为牌坊,下图为博物馆外貌。

Nestled in Wen-ming Road. Built up and opened to the general public in 1959, considered as a provincial-level comprehensive museum. Engaged in seeking, collecting cultural relics and specimen, conducting scientific research and launching exhibitions and displays with characteristics of different regions. The "Exhibition of Fine Collections in the Museum" displays those fine ceramics, Shi-wan colored pottery that was made in different parts of China between the Neolithic Age and Ming & Qing Dynasties. The upper picture shows the archway, and the lower picture shows the exterior look of the museum.

书院场馆

黄埔村
Huang-pu Village

位于海珠区,古代称为"凤洲",又称"凤浦",后由于外国人发音不准等缘故,此处被讹称为黄埔至今。清康熙时这里商船云集,一派繁华。至同治年间,由于水道日渐淤浅影响海船进出,曾停泊过瑞典"哥德堡号"、美国"中国皇后号"、澳大利亚"哈斯丁号"等外国商船的黄埔古港因此衰落。黄埔村不但见证了"古代海上丝绸之路"的世代繁盛,还产生过胡旋泽、冯肇宪等大批在中国近现代史上有重要影响的人物,因此有独一无二的历史地位。上图为古港码头,其余各图为村中景致。

Nestled in Hai-zhu District, previously called "Feng Zhou" or "Feng Pu" in ancient times. Owing to mistaken pronunciation by foreigners, this village was called Huang-pu until today. In the Kang Xi Emperor Reign of Qing Dynasty, there were a great number of commercial vessels calling here. In the Tong Zhi Emperor Reign, as the waterway transportation gained a decreasing popularity, the ancient Huang-pu Port, where a number of foreign commercial vessels were usually moored, went downhill progressively. As a matter of fact, Huang-pu Village has not only witnessed the generation-by-generation prosperity of the "ancient marine silk road", but also housed a galaxy of influential figures with great influences on the country's latter-day history, such as Hu Ze-xuan and Feng Zhao-xian, etc. Therefore, the village is of unprecedented historical values. The upper picture shows the ancient wharf, while the other pictures show different scenes in the village.

坑背—莲塘村
Keng-bei Lotus Pond Village

广州市第一批历史文化保护区之一，位于增城中新镇，始建于明代，重修于清代，古村落保存完好，能反映出明清两代的建筑风格，较完整地体现这一历史时期的传统风貌特色，是迄今为止我市发现的原始规划最完善、保存最完整的古村落。村前为半月形风水塘、胸围墙、门楼、晒谷场、街前路，依次排列着纵横巷、祠堂、书房、村屋，最后是用于防范匪贼，可储备粮食，固守待援的碉楼、后山及山林绿化。莲塘村离坑背村约1.5公里，是明代从莲塘村分迁出来的。上图为坑背村全貌，下右图为莲塘村。

Among the first group of protected areas for historical and cultural values in the city of Guangzhou. Nestled in Zhong-xin Town of Zeng-cheng, initially constructed in Ming Dynasty, and re-constructed in Qing Dynasty. The ancient village has been preserved in good condition, and can manifest the architectural styles of Ming and Qing Dynasties to the fullest extent. Considered as the best laid-out and protected block of ancient houses in today's Guangzhou. In front of the village, there is a lune-shaped Good Fortune Pond, enclosure wall, gate tower, grain basking yard, front road, Zong-heng lane, temple, study house, and villager's houses, etc, followed by a blockhouse which prevents thieves and bandits invision, and can be used to store cereals and grain; on top of that, the mountain has been covered by trees and greenery belts. The Lotus Pond Village is about 1.5 kilometers away from Keng-bei Village (which was in fact a branch of the Lotus Pond Village in Ming Dynasty). The upper picture shows the panorama of the Keng-bei Village, and the lower picture on the right shows the Lotus Pond Village.

古村寨

钟楼村
Bell Tower Village

广州市第一批历史文化保护区之一,位于从化神岗,建于清同治年间。村建在山麓与平地之间的缓冲处,布局、规划都是古建筑群中的佳作。村座西北向东南,以欧阳仁山公祠为轴线,左4巷,右3巷。村落建有城墙和既有防护、排洪作用,又兼分界、风水及美学功能的护城河。村中花岗岩砌边、青砖铺底的古排水渠今天仍在发挥作用。上图为钟楼村远眺,其余各图为村景。

Among the first group of protected areas for historical and cultural values in the city of Guangzhou. Nestled in Shen-gang of Cong-hua, initially constructed in the Tong-zhi Emperor Reign of Qing Dynasty. The village lies on a juncture area between the foot of mountain and a flat land, and has been laid out in a wholesome manner. The village faces southeastwards, and takes the Ou-yang-Ren-shan Temple as its axis line; there are 4 lanes on the left and 3 lanes on the right. The village is also furnished with a city wall, which could not only play a protector role and help discharge flood water, but also serve as a prefect foil to the overall scene. The ancient water discharge canals, which are covered by blue bricks and granite, are still working today. The upper picture shows the bird's view of the Bell Tower Village, and the other pictures show different scenes of the village.

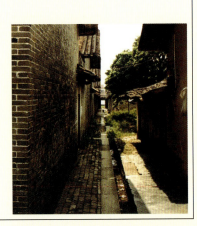

松柏堂
Pine and Cypress Hall

广州市第一批历史文化保护区之一，位于从化，建于清代，规划整齐划一，所有古建筑坐北朝南，砖、木、石结构，呈算盘状排列，是我市目前发现规模最大、价值较高的传统建筑群。村前一口大池塘，中间有苍劲挺拔的柏树，点出了"松柏堂"之题；每座民居天井都有水井，井水清澈长年不断。学宫原规模宏大，有宫墙、牌楼、泮池等，经过战乱，大部分设施已遭破坏。上图为松柏堂全貌。

Among the first group of protected areas for historical and cultural values in the city of Guangzhou. Nestled in Cong-hua, initially constructed in Qing Dynasty and laid out in a well-structured manner. All the ancient architectural structures face southwards, and are made of brick, wood and stone structures, being arranged in an abacus-like shape. Known as the largest and most valuable block of ancient architecture in today's Guangzhou. There is a large pond in front of the village, in which there grows a robust cypress. Each household has a well, from which clear water is available throughout the year. Originally, the Hall covered a large area, and was endued with a number of structures, such as adornment walls, archways, and ponds, etc., most of which were unfortunately destroyed by gunfire. The upper picture shows the panorama of the Hall.

古村寨

小洲村
Xiao-zhou Village

广州市第一批历史文化保护区之一,位于海珠区,始建于元末,街巷多为青石板铺砌,村内外水网密布,周边有大面积果林,是目前我市城区内发现的最具岭南水乡特色的古村寨。村有古码头登瀛码头;古桥娘马桥、细桥和翰墨桥;有众多古树,其中一株秋枫经鉴定为省内最古老的一株。村里保留了多间古民居和有沿海特色的蚝屋,保留了古朴的民风民俗、刺绣工艺等。下左图为古秋枫,中右图为村民做刺绣,其余各图为村景。

Among the first group of protected areas for historical and cultural values in the city of Guangzhou. Nestled in Hai-zhu District, initially constructed in the late period of Yuan Dynasty. Most streets and lanes in here are covered by bluestone blocks. There is a crisscross of waterways and rivers inside and outside the village; in the vicinity of the village, there are large areas of orchards. Considered as the earliest discovered ancient village characterized by the architectural style of Ling-nan Watery Region in the downtown area of Guangzhou. Inside the village, there are an ancient wharf (Deng Ying Wharf), an ancient bridge (Niang-ma Bridge), and two other bridges (Xi Bridge and Han Mo Bridge); many ancient trees; among others, an autumn maple has been proven to be the oldest one of its kind in the entire province. Besides, the village has preserved many ancient residential houses and oyster-shaped mansions that bear typical traits of coastal architecture; inside these houses and mansions, there are simple and ancient folk arts and embroidery works, etc. The lower picture on the left shows the ancient autumn maple tree, and the middle picture on the right shows the embroidering scene of villagers, and the other pictures show other scenes in the village.

古村寨

广裕祠
Guang-yu Ancestral Temple

位于从化太平镇,据传南宋宰相陆秀夫殉国后,其南迁族人逃到此处藏匿,广裕祠就是陆氏家族宗祠。陆氏后人最引为自豪的是他们祠堂上的"诗书开越,忠孝传家"8个字,上联指的是西汉陆贾说南越王赵佗归汉,下联意为南宋陆秀夫精忠报国之事。广裕祠堂荣获了2003年联合国教科文组织文化遗产保护竞赛"亚太地区文化遗产保护杰出项目奖第一名"。据悉,这是中国的文化遗产首度获得这一荣誉。

Nestled in Tai-ping Town of Cong-hua District. It was said that, after Lv Xiu-fu, the prime minister of Southern Song Dynasty, died for his country, his clansmen moved southwards and hid themselves in here. Guang-yu Temple was also the temple of Lv' s clansmen. The descendants of Lv' s clansmen were most proud of the eight Chinese characters on the tablet in their temple. As a matter of fact, the Guang-yu Temple turned out the winner of the first prize in the "Competition among Cultural Relics in Asia Pacific Region in Terms of Outstanding Protection Works" organized by UNESCO in 2003, thus becoming the very first cultural relic in China that won such a great honor.

聚龙村
Ju-long Village

广州市第一批历史文化保护区之一，位于芳村，现存二十一座两层青砖瓦楼房，是目前为止已知我市城区内最早实行整体规划并保存最完整的古村落。光绪年间，原籍广东台山的邝氏三兄弟买此地建成新村，共有20户从台山迁居于此。因建村挖土时冒出红朱岩石水，风水先生称为"龙出血"而得"聚龙"名。村中出了不少名人，如清末富商邝伍臣、"黄金巨子"邝衡石等。上图为聚龙村远眺，中右图为门饰。

Among the first group of protected areas for historical and cultural values in the city of Guangzhou. Nestled in Fang-cun District. Currently hosts 21 two-storeyed mansions made of blue bricks and tiles, known as the best developed ancient village, which has been planned out in a comprehensive way and at the earliest time, in today's Guangzhou that has come to knowledge of the local people. During the Guang Xu Emperor Reign, 3 Kuang-surnamed brothers who were born in Tai-shan of Guangdong province bought this piece of land to erect this village; at that time, a total of 20 families moved from Tai-shan to live in this village. This village was also termed as "Dragon Luck Village", for red water was exposed during the earth cutting course. The village has been the hometown of many personages, such as the business tycoon Kuang Wu-chen in the late period of Qing Dynasty, and Kuang Heng-shi, a tycoon of gold supplies. The upper picture shows a bird's view of the village, and the middle picture on the right shows the adornments on the door.

古村寨

王道夫祠堂
Wang-dao-fu ancestral temple

位于东圃大马路，重修于清乾隆六十年，为传统的砖木结构，两廊三厅两天井，石阶两旁有石栏，上雕花瓶、葫芦等图案。王道夫，广东南海人，南宋咸淳四年进士，后为南宋末年广州转运使、兵部尚书，曾率兵抗元。宋亡，王道夫愤恨而卒，其后人在此地为他建立了祠堂。上中图为祠堂匾额，下图为祠堂外貌。

Nestled in Da-ma Road of Dong-pu, reconstructed in the 60th year of Qian-long Emperor Reign of Qing Dynasty. Made of a traditional brick and wood structure, with 2 corridors, 3 halls and 2 patios. There are stone guardrails, which bear vase and calabash patterns on their surfaces, beside the stone staircases. Wang Dao-fu, born in Nan-hai of Guangdong Province, became a successful candidate in the highest imperial examinations in the 4th year of Xian-Chun Emperor Reign of Southern Song Dynasty, and was later appointed to take charge of transportation and military affairs in Guangzhou in the late period of Southern Song Dynasty. He once led troops to fight against the Yuan Army. When Song Dynasty was overthrown, Wang Do-fu died in resentment; his descendants set up a temple for him in here. The upper picture shows the horizontal tablet in the temple, and the lower picture shows the exterior look of the temple.

名人遗迹

明绍武君臣墓
Mausoleum of Emperor and High Officials in Shao-wu Reign of Ming Dynasty

位于越秀山。明隆武二年，明宗室南下广州重建政权，不足40天，清兵攻陷广州，君臣十五人被俘就义。此为绍武皇帝与臣子的合葬墓。

Nestled in Yue-xiu Mount. In the 2nd year of Long-wu Emperor Reign of Ming Dynasty, Ming Zong-shi went to Guangzhou to re-establish his powers. Within no more than 40 days, the troops of Qing Army occupied Guangzhou, 15 persons, including the Emperor and his high officials, were arrested and killed. This mausoleum has housed the bodies of Shao Wu Emperor and his ministers.

名人遗迹

明虎贲将军王兴墓
Tomb of A General Named Wang Xing in Ming Dynasty

位于越秀山。王兴（1615-1659），广东恩平人，明末率众奋起抗清，颇有战绩。当时逃亡肇庆的明永历皇帝朱由榔闻讯，赐王兴"虎贲将军"封号。

Nestled in Yue-xiu Mount. Wang Xing (1615-1659) was born in En-ping of Guangdong Province. In the late period of Ming Dynasty, he led the multitude to rise up against the then ruling government of Qing Dynasty, and achieved substantial victories. The then Long-li Emperor of Ming Dynasty, Zhu You-lang who was fleeing from royal palace, conferred the title of general to Wang Xing.

曾豫斋墓
Zeng Yu-zhai's Tomb

位于小谷围，据残存墓碑记述，墓主曾裕斋，赐进士奉政大夫福建按察司佥事，葬于明万历十八年。该墓为广州地区所知规模最大的石砌山手形明代墓葬，其石构件琢刻精美，前所未见，有较高历史价值和艺术价值。Nestled in the Xiao-gu-wei town. According to the historical record stated on the gravestone, the man within the tomb, Zeng Yu-zhai, was a high official in Fujian province, an buried in here in the 18th year of the Wan-li period of Ming Dynasty. This tomb is the largest one of stone structure in the entire region of Guangzhou, and features exquisite sculpting craftsmanship, consequently being of unprecedented high cultural and historical values.

刘氏家庙
Liu's Clan Temple

位于沙河大街,清末爱国将领刘永福于清光绪二十六年建造。刘参加过广西天地会起义,中法战争率领黑旗军在越南打击法国侵略者,中日甲午战争率军在台湾抗击日本侵略军,后回到广州沙河驻兵,民初任广东民团局总长。1906越南维新会以家庙为会址开展活动。上图为家庙外貌,其余各图为内外景致。

Nestled in Sha-he Avenue, erected by Liu Yong-fu, a patriotic general in the late period of Qing Dynasty, in the 26th year of Guang-xu Emperor Reign of Qing Dynasty. Liu ever took part in the Uprising organized by the Sky & Ground Society in Guangxi Province. In the China-France War, he led a Black-Banner Army to fight against French invaders in Vietnam. During the China-Japan Jia-wu War, he led an army to fight against Japanese invaders in Taiwan. Later, he returned to Guangzhou and was stationed at Sha-he; in the early period of the Republic of China (1912–1949), he served as the Director General for the Local Militia of Guangdong Province. In 1906, the Reform Society in Vietnam held activities in the site of this temple. The upper picture shows the exterior look of the temple, while the other pictures show the exterior and interior looks of the temple.

名人遗迹

邓氏宗祠
Deng's Clan Temple

位于宝岗路,为纪念民族英雄邓世昌而建立。1894年,日本挑起侵略中国的甲午战争。9月17日邓世昌在黄海海战中,率"致远"舰冲锋在前,英勇杀敌,座舰中弹将沉仍鼓轮直冲敌舰"吉野",欲与敌舰同归于尽。"致远"舰在途中沉没,邓世昌落海,虽遇救而不独生,为国壮烈捐躯。上图为宗祠外貌,中右图为邓世昌塑像,下右图为邓世昌手植的苹婆树。

Nestled in Bao-gang Road, erected to memorize Deng Shi-chang, a hero of the Chinese nation. In 1894, Japanese invaders waged a war to make inroads into China. On September 17 of that year, Deng Shi-chang commanded a "Zhi-yuan" titled vessel to fight against the Japanese invaders, and killed many enemies. Unfortunately, the vessel that Deng took was hit by a bomb; in spite of heavy risks, Deng ordered his soldiers to sail at full horsepower to collide with the enemy's vessel "Ji Ye". His vessel "Zhi Yuan" sank midway, Deng Shi-chang fell into the sea; after being saved, he opted for fighting further until losing his life at last. The upper picture shows the panorama of the temple, and the middle picture on the right shows the sculpture of Deng Shi-chang, and the lower picture on the right shows a stercoulia tree planted by Deng Shi-chang in person.

名人遗迹

屈大均墓
Qu Da-jun's Tomb

位于番禺新造。屈大均（1630～1696），字翁山。番禺人。明清学者、诗人。康熙十二年吴三桂反清，他入湘投军，察觉吴三桂不可为大事后，托病归故里，隐居著述，郁郁辞世。著述有《广东新语》、《翁山诗略》等30余种。

Nestled in Xin-zao Town of Panyu. Qu Da-jun (1630-1696), with his style name being Weng-shan, was born in Panyu. Known as a scholar and poet in the Ming and Qing Dynasties. In the 12th year of the Kang-xi Emperor Reign, Wu San-gui rose up in order to overthrow the then Qing Dynasty. Qu went to Hunan and joined the army, and dealt with Wu San-gui for a period of time, before finding out that Wu was not the right person to work with. Then Qu claimed that he was ill and came back to his hometown to live in seclusion. Later, he passed away in depression, after writing a series of books. Among others, his over 30 publications include "New Annals of Guangdong Province" "Weng Shan's Poems", etc.

资政大夫祠
Political Advisor's Temple

位于新华镇，清同治年兵部郎中徐方正为其祖父徐德魁封赠资政大夫而建，祠堂的建筑工艺精细讲究，水磨青砖墙，打磨地板砖，上盖陶瓦，山墙起锅耳，屋脊嵌立体和浮雕陶塑，檐下还有砖雕和木刻等。建筑虽受到损坏，但仍可窥其昔日的宏大堂皇。祠中最具历史文物价值的是天井内的圣旨牌坊。上图为祠堂全貌，下右图为牌坊，其余各图为内外景致。

Nestled in Xin-hua Town. Xu Fang-zheng, an advisor in the Department of War in the Tong-zhi Emperor Reign of Qing Dynasty had this temple erected to celebrate the event that his grandfather, Xu De-kui, was promoted to serve as a Political Advisor for the then State Government. The architectural structure of the temple is exquisite and tasteful and features a combination of blue brick walls and fine floor tiles, with ceramic tiles on the roofing too. Besides, the temple has housed a galaxy of brick sculpture and wood sculpture work-pieces. The most valuable relic is the Archway that bears the instructions given by a feudal emperor. The upper picture shows the panorama of the temple, and the lower picture on the right shows the archway, and the other pictures show the interior and exterior scenes of the temple.

名人遗迹

云从龙墓
Tomb of Yun Cong-long

位于沙河镇。云从龙，蒙古族人，在宋代景定举孝廉，壬戌登进士，元代授宣武将军湖广邕州安抚使、怀远大将军、广东琼州安抚使、昭勇大将军海北广东道提刑按察使、征南大将军等职，元贞二年病逝，御旨赐葬白云山。

Nestled in Sha-he Town. Yun Cong-long was of Mongolian nationality. He passed the feudal exam to become a state official in Song Dynasty. Later in Yuan Dynasty, he took a series of high positions in the then State government. He died in the 2nd year of the Yuan Zhen Period, and his body was buried in the Bai-yun Mount, according to the order of the then Emperor.

古应芬墓
Tomb of Gu Ying-fen

位于白云区东坑，碑文为胡汉民所撰。古应芬（1873-1931），广东梅县人，辛亥革命后任广东军政府秘书长。北代时期任大本营财政部长，国民政府财政部长等职。民国20年，古应芬曾联同邓泽如等发出弹劾蒋介石的提案。

Nestled at Dong Keng in Bai-yun District. The words on the inscription tablet were written by Hu Han-min. Gu Ying-fen 1873-1931 was born at Mei County of Guangdong Province. After the 1911 Revolution, he acted as the Secretary General for the Military Government of Guangdong Province. In the Northern Expedition period, he served as the Financial Minister at the headquarters, and the Financial Minister of the then national People's Government. In the 20th year of the Republic of China times (1012-1949), Gu Ying-fen once collaborated with Deng Ze-ru, etc. to put forward a bill to impeach Chiang Kai-shek.

伍廷芳纪念像
Wu Ting-fang Memorial Figure

位于越秀山。伍廷芳（1842-1922），广东新会人。历任清驻美等国大使、外交部右侍郎。辛亥革命后任司法、外交总长、代总理。1922年任广东省省长。右上图为墓园。Nestled in Yue-xiu Mount. Wu Ting-fang (1842-1922) was born in Xin-hui of Guangdong Province. He ever served as the Ambassador to USA of the Chinese Government in Qing Dynasty, and an official in the then Department of Foreign Affairs. After the 1911 Revolution, Wu served as the Head for the then Juridical Department and Director General and Acting Head for the then Department of Foreign Affairs in succession. In 1922, he became the governor of Guangdong. The upper picture on the right shows the Tomb Park.

名人遗迹

仲元楼
Zhong-yuan Tower

位于越秀山。邓仲元（1886-1922），广东惠阳人，参加过黄花岗起义，曾任广东军政府陆军司司长，参加过讨袁、驱除龙济光等战役，功绩卓著。Nestled in Yue-xiu Mount. Deng Zhong-yuan (1886-1922) was born in Hui-yang of Guangdong Province. He participated in the Huang-hua-gang Uprising, and served as Head for the Department of Land Army of the Military Government of Guangdong, and took part in the fight against the warlords Yuan Shi-kai and the fight for booting out Long Ji-guang, etc. He attained brilliant military accomplishments.

朱执信墓
Tomb of Zhu Zhi-xin

位于先烈东路。朱执信（1885-1920），生于广东番禺。早年加入同盟会，曾参加黄花岗起义和讨代袁世凯等斗争。曾任中华革命军广东司令官等职。

Nestled in Xian-lie Road East. Zhu Zhi-xin (1885-1920) was born in Panyu of Guangdong Province. At an early age, he joined the Chinese Revolutionary League, and participated in the Huang-hua-gang Uprising and the fight against the warlord Yuan Shi-kai. He once served as the Commander for Guangdong Military Region of the then Chinese People's Revolutionary Army.

胡汉民墓
Tomb of Hu Han-min

位于广汕公路。胡汉民（1879-1936），广东番禺人。早年参加同盟会，历任广东都督、南京国民政府主席、立法院院长、国民党中央常务委员会主席。

Nestled in Guangzhou-Shantou Road. Hu Han-min (1879-1936) was born in Panyu of Guangdong Province. At an early age, he joined the Chinese Revolutionary League, and served as governor of Guangdong province, Chairman of the National People's Government in Nanjing, President for the then Legislative Body, and Chairman for the Central Standing Committee of Kuomintang in succession.

陈济棠公馆
Chen Ji-tang's Residence

位于梅花村。1931-1936年，陈济棠治粤时在此建公馆，并在附近广植梅花。每逢寒冬时节梅花吐艳，芬芳扑鼻，故俗称为梅花村。陈济棠故居现为省妇联办公地，旧貌依存。陈济棠（1890-1954），防城人。历任粤军营长、团长、旅长等职务，1931年起至1935年全面掌握广东军政大权，采取措施发展近代经济，成效显著。上图为公馆主楼，其余各图为公馆外部景致。

Nestled in the Plum Tree Village. Between 1931 and 1936, Chen Ji-tang, when he was serving as the governor of Guangdong province, has a residence of his own erected. Chen also had some plum trees planted nearby his residence. Thus, the local village was called "Plum Tree Village". The former residence of Chen Ji-tang has now become the office premises of Guangdong Provincial Women's Federation, and been preserved in good condition. Chen Ji-tang (1890-1954), was born in Fang-cheng, and served as battalion head, colonel, brigadier, etc. in succession. Since 1931 and until 1935, he took charge of the military powers of Guangdong province on the whole, and employed measures to develop the economic potentialities of Guangdong, attaining great accomplishments. The upper picture shows the main mansion of the residence, and the other pictures show the exterior scenes of the residence.

名人遗迹

陈树人纪念馆
Chen Shu-ren Memorial Hall

位于署前路10号。明清时期，岭南画派著名画家陈树人在此兴建楟园。该园毁于战火。后再建栎园，楼下为客厅、画厅及饭厅。现此地辟为纪念馆。

Nestled at No.10 Shu-qian Road. In Ming and Qing Dynasties, Chen Shu-ren, a renowned painter of Ling-nan (i.e. the south of the Five Ridges, the area covering Guangdong and Guangxi Provinces) style, ever embarked on a park called "Chu House" in here, which was unfortunately destroyed by gunfire. Later, Chen had another park called "Le House" erected. There is a living room, a painting room and a dining room downstairs. Nowadays, the Le House has been expanded to be a memorial hall.

名人遗迹

赵少昂岭南艺苑旧址
Relics of Zhao Shao-ang Ling-Nan Artistic School

位于十甫路湛露直街24号，是典型的西关竹筒屋，是著名的岭南画家赵少昂先生民国时期讲学传艺之所。

Nestled at No.24 Zhan Lu Zhi Street, Shi-pu Road. Known as a typical bamboo structured architecte of the "western downtown of Guangzhou" style. Mr. Zhao Shao-ang, a famed painter of Ling-nan (i.e. the south of the Five Ridges, the area covering Guangdong and Guangxi Provinces) style taught and delivered speeches to his students during the period of the Republic of China (1912-1949).

廖仲恺、何香凝纪念馆
Memorial Hall of Liao Zhong-kai and He Xiang-ning:

位于纺织路,是一座砖木结构的二层楼,原是何香凝1927年3月创办的仲恺农工学校的办事处旧址。廖仲恺、何香凝夫妇是我国近代民主革命著名的政治活动家,他们追随孙中山从事推翻清王朝的革命活动,参加过讨袁,促成第一次国共合作等。上图为纪念馆外貌,下左图为廖仲恺纪念碑,下右图为何香凝在仲恺学校中的塑像。

Nestled in the Fang-zhi Road, known as a brick-&-wood 2-storeyed mansion. The site of this Hall used to be occupied by the office premises of the Zhong-kai Peasants and Workers Training School embarked on by He Xiang-ning in March 1927. As husband and wife, Liao Zhong-kai and He Xiang-ning were both renowned political activists in China's latter-day history of democratic revolution. They followed after the steps of Sun Yat-sen to overthrow the feudal Qing Dynasty, and participated in the fight against the warlord Yuan Shi-kai, as well as played an active part in facilitating the first ever cooperation between the Chinese Communist Party and Kuomintang. The upper picture shows the exterior look of the memorial hall, the lower picture on the left shows the Liao Zhong-kai Monument, and the lower picture on the right shows the sculpture of He Xiang-ning within Zhong-Kai School.

名人遗迹

鲁迅纪念馆
Lu Xun Memorial Hall

位于文明路。馆址所在地俗称钟楼。1927年1月，由中央广东区委推荐、中山大学聘请，鲁迅从厦门来广州任中山大学中文系主任兼教务主任，就住此处。展馆复原了鲁迅当年的居住环境，室内还有四方桌、小茶几和鲁迅亲笔书写了"L.S"（鲁迅二字的英文缩写）字样的藤箱。这些都是原物。上图为钟楼，中左图为鲁迅塑像，下右图为鲁迅使用过的家具。

Nestled in Wen-ming Road. The site of the hall used to be occupied by a Bell Tower. In January 1927, Lu Xun was recommended by the then Chinese Communist Party of Guangdong Province and invited by Zhong-shan University to come from Xiamen to teach in Zhong-shan University in Guangzhou. Lu Xun thus became the Dean of Zhongshan University and Director the Office for Educational Administration in the same university, and resided in here. The Memorial Hall exhibited the original residence in the place where Lu Xun resided, with all those items of Lu's own, such as the square table, small tea table, and the rattan box bearing the initials written by Lu Xun in person. The upper picture shows the Bell Tower, the middle picture on the left shows the sculpture of Lu Xun, and the lower picture on the right shows the furniture that Lu Xun ever used.

冼星海公墓
Memorial Park of Xian Xing-hai

位于麓湖公园。冼星海，生于1905年，广东番禺人，曾留学法国巴黎音乐学院，民国1935年回国参加抗日救亡运动，期间创作了500多首歌曲，其中有著名的《黄河大合唱》等。1945年10月病逝于莫斯科，毛泽东亲题悼词："为人民的音乐家冼星海同志致哀"。上图为星海园外貌，中左图为冼星海塑像，中右图为纪念馆。

Nestled in the Lu-hu Park. Xian Xing-hai was born in Panyu of Guangdong Province in 1905, and studied in the Paris Acadmy of Music in France. In 1935, he returned to China to play an active part in the Anti-Japanese-Invaders War, and composed over 500 songs during that time, inclusive of the nationwide renowned "Yellow River Chorus". Xian died in Moscow in October 1945. Chairman Mao Ze-dong lamented the passing of Xian Xing-hai by writing an inscription in person. The upper picture shows the exterior view of the memorial park, the middle park on the left shows the sculpture of Xian Xing-hai, and the middle picture on the right shows the memorial hall.

名人遗迹

清代炮台
Emplacement of Qing Dynasty

位于小谷围，据村民相传，为林则徐所建，为抗英的第三道防线。1717年以后，康熙下达南洋贸易禁令，为了对出海口进行全面封锁，沿海各地建筑了许多炮台，专家推测，此炮台为康熙石子头炮台。上图为残存的炮台基础，下图为整个炮台的鸟瞰图。
Nestled in the Xiao-gu-wei Town, initially established by order of Lin Ze-xu, according to the local villagers. Used to be the third line of defense against British invaders. After 1717, Emperor Kang Xi gave an order to ban the country's trading with the Southeast Asian countries. To blank off all those sea gates, many emplacements were set up in coastal regions of the then China. According to experts, this emplacement is of Shi-zi-tou type during the reign of Emperor Kang Xi. The upper picture shows the relic of the emplacement foundation, and the lower picture shows the bird's view of the entire emplacement.

近代史迹

三元古庙
Ancient Temple at San-yuan

位于广园路。1841年5月29日，一群英军闯入三元里骚扰，被韦绍光等村民击毙数人，并将其尸体投入猪屎坑内。村民为防英军报复，在此举行集会，决定武装抗击，103乡群众奋起响应。30日，英军再次进犯。义勇于牛栏岗奋勇杀敌，英军伤亡逾百人。此役揭开了近代中国人民反侵略斗争的序幕。上图为古庙外景，下右图为召集乡民时使用的大钟。

Nestled in Guang-yuan Road. On May 29 1841, a gang of British soldiers broke into San-yuan-li to incite molestation; some of them were shot down by Wei Shao-guang, and their bodies were thrown into a pig feces pit. The local villagers gathered together in here and decided to form armed forces to fight against the British power that was about to seek revenge. In fact, the general public in up to 103 townships echoed ardently to this gathering overnight. On the 30th day of 1841, the British soldiers invaded once again. The militia fought hand-to-hand against and killed nearly 100 British invaders. This combat was the very start of the Chinese people's fight against foreign invaders. The upper picture shows the exterior look of the ancient temple, and the lower picture on the right shows the big bell that was used to ring for gathering up the villagers.

石井桥
Stone Well Bridge

位于石井镇,建于清道光年间。1856年9月,英国军舰炮轰广州城,挑起第二次鸦片战争。期间石井人民在此进行武装抗击,现桥的石栏板上还留有当时侵略军炮击的弹洞。中图为桥旁的石马雕刻。

Nestled in the Stone Well Town, initially constructed in the Dao-guang Emperor Reign of Qing Dynasty. In September 1856, a British military warship launched a bombardment against Guangzhou, thus arousing the second Opium War. During that war, the local people living in the Stone Well Town formed armed forces to fight against British invaders. On the stone bridge with guardrails of the day, there still exist those holes of bullets. The middle picture shows the horse-shaped stone sculpture by the bridge.

三元里抗英纪念碑
Anti-British-Invaders Monument at San-yuan-li

位于广园路。是纪念1841年三元里人民反侵略武装抵御英军的英雄壮举而设立的纪念碑。纪念碑附近有辟作三元里人民抗英斗争纪念馆的三元古庙。

Nestled in Guang-yuan Road, established to memorize those heroes that fought bravely against the then British invaders who broke into San-yuan-li in 1841. In its vicinity, there exists an ancient San-yuan temple, which also serves as a memorial hall for these heroes in the eyes of Chinese people.

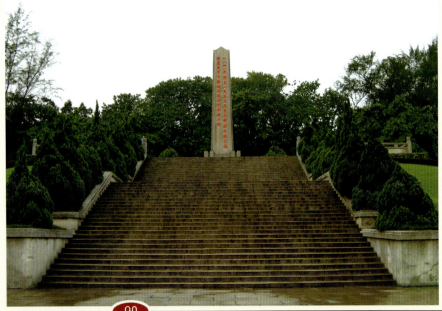

近代史迹

升平社学
Sheng-ping Society

位于石井镇。1841年三元里人民抗英斗争后,广州多个地方都有组织社学反侵略武装,由南海举人李芳等建立的升平社学是其中最早的社学之一。上左图为学社内部结构,上右图为大门匾额。

Nestled in the Stone Well Town. After the anti-British-invaders war in 1841, many local communities in Guangzhou organized societies to join in the armed forces for fighting against British invaders. The Sheng-ping Society, embarked on by Li Fang (born in Nan-hai of Guangdong Province), is one of those societies of this kind established at the earliest time. The upper picture on the left shows the interior scene of the society, and the upper picture on the right shows the horizontal tablet on the gate of the society.

近代史迹

义勇祠
Yi-yong Temple

位于石井镇,建于道光年间。咸丰四年该祠在战火中被毁,1866年重建。祠内现陈列着三元里抗英的有关图片,及当年牺牲的义勇名单等。

Nestled in the Stone Well Town, initially constructed during the Dao Guang Emperor Reign. In the 4th year of Xian-Feng Emperor's Reign, this temple was destroyed by a bombardment, and was not rebuilt up until 1866. Inside the temple of the day, there exist some photos reflecting the scenes where local people at San-yuan-li fought against British invaders, plus a name list of those Chinese people who lost their lives during that war.

洲头咀抗英纪念雕塑
Zhou-tou-zui Anti-British-Invaders Memorial Sculpture

位于滨江西路。1847 年 4 月，英军派军舰驶入珠江，妄图"恃强硬占"洲头咀土地。当地群众奋起抗威，10 多万市民纷纷支援，迫使英军打消了念头。

Nestled in Bin-jiang Road West. In April 1847, the British army sent a military warship to enter the Pearl River, in an attempt to occupy the land at Zhou-tou-zui by force. Over 100,00 local residents swarmed onto streets collectively to demonstrate their anger, which scared away British troops.

"沙基惨案"纪念碑
"Sha-ji Massacre" Monument

位于沙面。1925 年 6 月 23 日广州群众为声援上海人民反帝斗争举行了声势浩大游行示威，在沙基的英法军队公然向游行队伍开枪，造成了 100 多人死伤的惨案。

Nestled in Sha-mian. On June 23 1925, the multitude in Guangzhou organized a resounding parade to demonstrate their support for the Shanghai residents' fight against imperial invaders. The British and French soldiers stationed in Sha-ji had the afrontary to fire at the demonstrating people, causing over 100 demonstrators to die.

黄花岗起义指挥部旧址
Relics of the Commanding Headquarters during the Huang-hua-gang Uprising

位于越华路。1911年4月,孙中山领导的中国同盟会决定在广州发动武装起义,因这里距主攻目标两广总督署仅500米左右,位置上有近攻速取之利,因而起义的指挥部就设在这里。旧址有黄兴题的对联:"七十二健儿酣战春云湛碧血,四百兆国子愁看秋雨湿黄花。"旧址中有七十二烈士的生平简介、总督署的石狮子等。上左图为室内结构,下图为起义时使用过的物品。

Nestled in Yue-hua Road. In April 1911, the Chinese Revolutionary League led by Sun Yat-sen decided to launch an armed uprising in Guangzhou. The commanding headquarters was set up in here, because it was only 500 meters or so away from here to the office premises of the then governor of Guangdong and Guangxi provinces, the main target to fire at. There is a couplet written by Huang Xing here, expressing the local people's lamentation over those who lost their lives in the uprising. In addition, you can see the biographies of the 72 martyrs, and the stone lions in the governor's office premises. The upper picture on the left shows the interior structure, and the lower picture shows those articles that were ever used during the uprising.

近代史迹

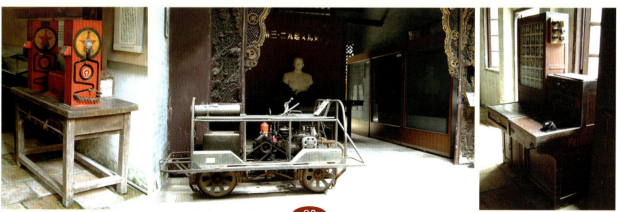

黄花岗七十二烈士陵园
Cemetery of 72 Martyrs at Huang-hua-gang

位于先烈中路,为纪念孙中山先生领导的同盟会在广州起义战役中牺牲的烈士而建。1911年4月27日孙中山领导的同盟会为推翻清王朝的统治,在广州举行起义,结果失败,喻培伦等英勇牺牲。同盟会会员潘达微,冒着生命危险把散落的七十二烈士遗骸收殓安葬于红花岗(后改为黄花岗,取菊花傲霜节操之意)。孙中山书浩气长存四字镌于墓坊。烈士墓的纪功坊峙立墓后,坊上的金字形叠石上端,自由神像高擎火炬,象征着烈士们为追求自由解放而死的献身精神。陵园曾为羊城八景景点之一。上图为烈士合葬墓坊,下左图为碑铭。

Nestled in Xian-lie Road Central, initially established to commemorate those martyrs who were members of the Chinese Revolutionary League headed by Sun Yat-sen, and lost their lives during the uprising in Guangzhou. On April 27 1911, the Chinese Revolutionary League headed by Sun Yat-sen launched an uprising in order to overthrow the feudal Qing Dynasty, which boiled down to a failure. As a result, Yu Pei-lun and other risers died. Pan Da-wei, a member with the Chinese Revolutionary League, risked his life to collect the bodies of 72 martyrs and bury them in the Hong-hua-gang (later renamed as Huang-hua-gang). Sun Yat-sen wrote an inscription for the 72 martyrs in person for lamentation. Behind the tomb of these martyrs, there lies a memorial archway, surmounted up by a figure of the God of Freedom, symbolizing the martyrs' ardent pursuit of liberty. This cemetery was listed as one of the eight major cultural attractions in the city of Guangzhou. The upper picture shows the archway on the tomb, and the lower picture shows the inscription.

黄花岗七十二烈士陵园
Cemetery of 72 Martyrs at Huang-hua-gang

上左图为各界人士为纪念烈士所立的石碑，上右图为著名民主革命家、出版家、美术家、摄影家、慈善家潘达微墓，他当时冒着危险安葬了黄花岗七十二烈士。

The upper picture on the left shows the stone monument established for the martyrs, the upper picture on the right shows the tomb of Pan Da-wei, a renowned democratic revolutionist, publisher, artist, photographer and charitarian. Pan risked his life to bury the 72 martyrs at Huang-hua-gang.

近代史迹

大元帅府旧址
Relics of the Marshal's Residence

位于纺织路。1917年至1924年,孙中山在广东建立革命政权,均以此地作为大元帅府。1917年孙中山南下护法,9月10日在此宣誓就职中华民国军政府大元帅,设大元帅府。孙的许多重大决策,如护法斗争、平息广州商团叛乱、改组国民党、促成第一次国共合作等都是在大元帅府内作出的。上图为大元帅府外貌,其余各图为府内外景致。

Nestled in Fang-zhi Road. From 1917 to 1924, Sun Yat-sen set up an organ of revolutionary political power in Guangdong province, and has a marshal's residence erected in here. In 1917, Sun Yat-sen visited Guangzhou and was sworn into office of Marshal for the Republic of China on September 10. Sun made many of his significant decisions in this residence. The upper picture shows the exterior look of the residence, and the other pictures show different scenes inside and outside the residence.

近代史迹

国民党 "一大" 旧址
Relics of the "First Congress of Kuomintang"

位于文明路，是第一次国共合作的诞生地。1924年1月20日至30日，孙中山在这里主持召开了国民党 "一大"，改组国民党，制定联俄联共扶助农工三大政策等。共产党人李大钊、毛泽东、林伯渠、瞿秋白等参加了这次大会的领导工作，并且当选为中国国民党第一届中央执行委员和候补中央执行委员。上图中礼堂里的23号、39号分别是李大钊和毛泽东当时所坐的位置。下左图为钟楼，中图为孙中山与李大钊塑像。

Nestled in Wen-ming Road, known as where the meeting that facilitated the first ever cooperation between the Chinese Communist Party and Kuomintang was held. From the 20th day to the 30th day of January in 1924, Sun Yat-sen held and presided over the first ever congress of Kuomintang, reorganized the Kuomintang and formulated three major policies (i.e. uniting with Russia, uniting with the Communist forces worldwide and offering support to peasants and workers as well). Those important figures, such as Li Da-zhao, Mao Ze-dong, Lin Bo-qu, and Qu Qiu-bai, etc, have all attended this congress, and were also elected the Executive Members and Alternate Members with the Central Committee of the Very First Congress of Kuomintang. The upper picture shows the seats No. 23 and No. 39, which were respectively taken up by Li Da-zhao and Mao Ze-dong. The lower picture on the left shows the bell tower, and the middle picture shows the sculptures of Sun Yat-sen and Li Da-zhao.

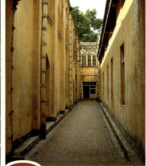

黄埔军校
Huang-pu Military Academy

位于黄埔区长洲岛，广州市第一批历史文化保护区之一的"长洲镇"中的主要景点，在我国近代史上有极高的知名度，是第一次国共合作时期，孙中山在中国共产党和苏联的帮助下创办的新型陆军军官学校，在这里曾培养了大批著名的国、共两党将领。黄埔军校是广州作为革命策源地最重要的体现之一。现存的景点有校本部、孙中山故居、东征烈士墓和纪念碑等。上图为校本部外貌，下图为长洲岛远眺，其余各图为军校内外景致。

Nestled on the Chang-zhou Island of Huang-pu District, listed among the first group of protected areas for historical and cultural values in the capacity of a major attraction on Chang-zhou Town. Enjoys a rather high fame in the latter-day history of China. During the period of the first ever cooperation between Kuomintang and the Chinese Communist Party, Sun Yat-sen embarked on a military academy with supports conferred by the Chinese Communist Party and the then Soviet Union, where a galaxy of renowned generals were trained up for both the Chinese Communist Party and Kuomintang. This academy is considered as one of the most powerful proofs that testify that Guangzhou is a revolutionary base. Inside the academy of the day, there exist such attractions as the headquarters, former residence of Sun Yat-sen, tomb of those martyrs who lost their lives in the Eastern Expedition, and a monument, etc. The upper picture shows the exterior look of the headquarters, the lower picture shows a bird's view of Chang-zhou Island, and the other pictures show the exterior and interior scenes of the academy.

近代史迹

中华全国总工会旧址
Relics of All-China Federation of Trade Unions

位于越秀南路，这里原为中国国民党中央党部所在地。1924年国民党"一大"结束后，国民党中央党部即在二楼办公。广州工人代表大会则设在一楼。中央党部农民部主办的农民运动讲习所第一、二届就在天台的临时建筑内举办。1925年10月，中华全国总工会从大德路迁入这里二楼办公。上图为旧址外貌，下左图为廖仲恺牺牲纪念碑。

Nestled in Yue-xiu Road South, used to be the site of the headquarters of the Central Committee of Kuomintang. After the first congress of Kuomintang ended in 1924, the headquarters of the Central Committee of Kuomintang had its office set up on the 2nd floor. Guangzhou Workers' Representative Congress had its office set up on the first floor. The first and second study sessions of the Peasant Movement Vacation School launched by the Peasants Management Department of the Central Committee of the Chinese Communist Party were launched within the temporarily erected buildings on the terrace. In October 1925, All-China Federation of Trade Unions relocated itself from Da-de Road onto the 2nd floor. The upper picture shows the outlook of the relics, and the lower picture on the left shows the Liao Zhong-kai Monument.

近代史迹

毛泽东同志主办农民运动讲习所旧址
Relics of Peasant Movement Vacation School embarked on by Comrade Mao Ze-dong

位于中山四路，原址为番禺学宫。"农讲所"在国共合作时期共举办了六届，先后由彭湃、毛泽东等主持。肖楚女、周恩来等任教员。来自全国各地的学生经过培训，毕业后奔赴各地领导农民开展反帝反封建斗争，为中国革命作出了重大的贡献。上图为农讲所外貌，中左图为青年毛泽东塑像，下左、中图为毛泽东当年起居的房子。

Nestled in Zhong-shan No. 4 Road, used to be the site of Panyu Study Hall. The vacation school had in total 6 study sessions launched during the period of cooperation between the Chinese Communist Party and Kuomintang; such sessions were presided over by Peng Bai and Mao Ze-dong in succession; and Xiao Chu-n and Zhou En-lai served as teachers. Students hailing from all cross the country were trained up and sent to different parts of the country after graduation, thus to lead the peasants in the whole country to fight against the feudal and imperial systems. This vacation school has contributed heavily to the evolvement of revolutionary movement in China. The upper picture shows the outlook of the vacation school, the middle picture on the left shows the sculpture of Mao Ze-dong (when he was young), and the lower picture and the middle picture on the left show the houses where Mao Ze-dong lived.

近代史迹

省港罢工委员会旧址
Relics of the Commanding Committee of the Guangdong and HK Strike

位于东园横路,原是清末广东水师提督李准的别墅。在省港罢工期间,是委员会所在地。1926年11月,大部分房子被反动分子焚毁,现仅存门楼。
Nestled in Dong-yuan-heng Road, used to be a villa where Li Zhun, provincial commander-in-chief in charge of the navy in Guangdong province in the late period of Qing Dynasty, lived. During the period of Guangdong and HK Strike, the commanding committee was located here. In November 1926, most of the houses were burnt down by reactionaries. Nowadays, only the gate tower is preserved.

广东省农民协会旧址
Relics of Guangdong Provincial Peasants' Association

位于东皋大道。1925年1月,广州农民运动讲习所从越秀南路迁到这里续办第三至第五届。同年5月,广东省农民协会成立,办公地就设于此。
Nestled in Dong-Gao Avenue. In January 1925, Guangzhou Peasant Movement Vacation School was relocated from Yue-xiu Road South to here, to have its 3rd–5th sessions launched in here. In May of the same year, Guangdong Provincial Peasants' Association was established, and had its office set up in here.

广州公社旧址
Relics of Guangzhou Commune

位于起义路。1927年12月11日，中国共产党在广州发动了武装起义，工农赤卫队和革命军人迅速占领了广州市公安局，并在这里成立广州苏维埃政府。这个被世人誉为"东方的巴黎公社"的苏维埃政权虽仅存在三天，但在中国革命的历史上写下了光辉一页。旧址有《广州起义史料陈列室》。

Nestled in Qi-yi Road. On December 11 1927, the Chinese Communist Party launched an army uprising in Guangzhou. The workers and peasants' forces and revolutionary soldiers occupied Guangzhou City Public Security Bureau quickly, and established the Soviet Government of Guangzhou in here. Although this Soviet Power, which was famed as "Paris Commune in the Orient", remained in force for only 3 days, it had a far-reaching influence on the country's history of revolution. There is a "Display Room of Historical Materials about Guangzhou Uprising" in here.

十九路军淞沪抗日阵亡将士陵园
Cemetery of those military officials and soldiers of the 19th Route Army who lost their lives in the Song-hu war against Japanese invaders

位于先烈东路,为纪念国民革命军第十九路军在1932年"一·二八"淞沪抗日战役中阵亡将士,于1933年由华侨捐资建成。陵园有凯旋门、先烈纪念碑、英名碑、抗日亭、将士墓、战士墓、先烈纪念馆等七处烈士纪念建筑物。建筑规模宏伟,布局严谨,造型庄重典雅,主体建筑均用花岗石砌成。下左图为凯旋门,其余各图为陵园内外景致。

Nestled in Xian-lie Road East, initially constructed in 1933 by use of money donated by overseas Chinese, in an aim to commemorate those military officials and soldiers of the 19th route army of the National People's Revolutionary Force who lost their lives in the Song-hu war against Japanese invaders on January 28 of 1932. There are 7 architectural structures in commemoration of martyrs inside the cemetery, inclusive of the Triumphal Arch, Martyr Memorial Monument, Heroes' Name List Monument, Anti-Japanese Pavilion, Tomb of Officials, Tomb of Soldiers, and Martyrs Memorial Hall, etc. The architecture in here looks splendid and solemn, with the main architectural structure built up by use of granite. The lower picture on the left shows the Triumphal Arch, and the other pictures show the exterior and interior scenes of the cemetery.

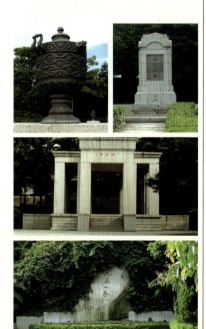

中共"三大"旧址
Relics of the Venue of the 3rd Congress of the Chinese Communist Party

位于新河浦路。1923年6月，中共"三大"召开，中国共产党中央机关迁到广州，春园即为党中央的活动地，陈独秀、李大钊、毛泽东等也住在这里，并在此修改中国共产党党纲、党章，起草大会宣言和各项决议草案。上图为春园原址，下右图为春园旁的葵园，它的楼顶有"1922"字样，是参加"三大"的代表的认路路标。

Nestled in Xin-he-pu Road. In June 1923, the Chinese Communist Party held its "3rd congress", and relocated its office premises to Guangzhou. The Spring Garden hosted the office premises of the Central Committee of the Chinese Communist Party; while Chen Du-xiu, Li Da-zhao, and Mao Ze-dong lived and amended the program, articles of association of the Chinese Communist Party, drafted the declaration for the congress and worked out the drafts of different resolutions in here. The upper picture shows the relics of the Spring Garden, the lower picture on the right shows the Sunflower Garden by Spring Garden. There is an inscription "1922" at the top of the building, which was written to facilitate those delegates to the 3rd congress to find the building easily.

近代史迹

中共广东区委会旧址
Relics of the Guangdong Provincial Committee of the Chinese Communist Party

位于文明路。1924-1927年间，中共广东区委员会曾在此办公。当年党的机关未公开，使用"管东渠"（"广东区"的谐音）的化名向警察局登记。周恩来、熊雄、彭湃、阮啸仙、刘尔崧、董平、邓中夏、蔡畅、邓颖超、区梦觉、张太雷、恽代英等人曾在此办公。《少年先锋》、《中国青年》等刊物曾在此编辑。上左图为旧址外貌。

Nestled in Wen-ming Road. Between 1924 and 1927, the Guangdong Provincial Committee of the Chinese Communist Party had its office established in here. At that time, the office organ of the Chinese Communist Party was not made public, but registered in the name of Guan Dong-qu (a pun to Guangdong Region) with the Police Bureau. Zhou En-lai, Xiong Xiong, Peng Bai, Yuan Xiao-xian, Liu Er-song, Dong Ping, Deng Zhong-xia, Cai Chang, Deng Ying-chao, Ou Meng-jue, Zhang Tai-lei, and Hui Dai-ying all worked in here. Besides, this site once acted as the editorial office for the publications such as "Pioneer Youth" and "Chinese Youth", etc. The upper picture on the left shows the outlook of the relics.

近代史迹

广州起义烈士陵园
Cemetery of Martyrs in Guangzhou Uprising

位于中山三路,为纪念广州起义中牺牲的烈士而建。1927年12月11日,在中共广东省委书记张太雷以及叶挺、叶剑英、苏兆征、聂荣臻、徐向前领导下,发动了广州起义,150多名朝鲜人和苏联驻广州领事馆人员也参加了起义。起义失败后有5700多人被惨遭杀害。此处曾为羊城八景景点之一。上图为烈士合葬陵墓,下左图为叶剑英纪念碑。

Nestled in Zhong-shan No. 3 Road, initially constructed in an aim to commemorate those martyrs who lost their lives in the Guangzhou Uprising. On December 11 1927, under leadership by Zhang Tai-lei (Secretary for the Chinese Communist Party in Guangdong Province), and other cadres (such as Ye Ting, Ye Jian-ying, Su Zhao-zheng, Nie Rong-zhen, and Xu Xiang-qian), Guangzhou Uprising was launched. Over 150 Koreans and some personnel with the Soviet Union's Consulate in Guangzhou also attended the uprising. After the uprising failed, over 5,700 persons were killed. This cemetery was once listed among the eight major cultural attractions in Guangzhou. The upper picture shows the tomb of martyrs, and the lower picture on the left shows the Ye Jian-ying Monument.

近代史迹

广东革命历史博物馆
Guangdong Revolutionary History Museum

位于陵园西路,是我省展示广东近百年来革命历史的专题博物馆。馆址原是清末广东咨议局旧址,建于宣统元年,辛亥革命后,广东人民在这里召开大会,宣布反清独立。1921年5月孙中山在此宣誓就任非常大总统,1996年成立广州近代史博物馆,两个馆牌同一馆舍,内容着重反映1840年至1949年广州各方面的历史概况。

Nestled in Ling-yuan Road West, known as a theme museum for exhibiting the revolutionary history of Guangzhou during the past century. The site of this museum used to be covered by Guangdong Consultation Bureau in the late period of Qing Dynasty, which was initially constructed in the first year of Xuan-tong Emperor Reign. After the 1911 revolution, people in Guangdong province held a congress in here to declare their waging war against the then feudal Qing Dynasty and claim for independence. In May 1921, Sun Yat-sen was sworn into office of Extraordinary President. In 1996, Guangzhou Latter-day History Museum was founded. The same hall bears two signboards. The articles in the museum reflect the historical scenarios in Guangzhou between 1840 and 1949.

近代史迹

迎春花市
Flower Market on the Eve of Spring Festival

广州又叫花城，其一年一度的迎春花市为世人所瞩目。市民除夕最重要的一个节目是逛花市。除夕前三天，许多地方搭起彩楼花架，四乡的花农和各地商家纷至沓来，售卖鲜花盆桔、年货精品，一时十里长街繁花似海，人潮如过江之鲫，直闹到大年初一凌晨，满载而归的人们方才尽兴散去。上图为2002年海珠花市，下图为2004年天河花市。
Guangzhou is called a floral city. The flower market on the eve of the Spring Festival in each year asrrests the attention of the multitude. In the Spring Festival, people in Guangzhou deem the flower market as the most important place to visit. By 3 days in advance of the Spring Festival, flower racks are put up here and there, flower growers and dealers from many different places swarm into the market to sell a rich diversity of fresh flowers, until the wee hours of the very first day of the new year, when people would come back to their homes with flowers in hands. The upper picture shows the snapshot of the flower market in Hai-zhu District in the Spring Festival of year 2002, and the lower picture shows the snapshot of the flower market in Tian-he District in the Spring Festival of year 2004.

民俗风情

沙湾飘色
Sha-wan Piao-se

飘色是戏剧、杂技和装饰艺术的糅合体。其构造是在一小块板上用小童担当演员,将其安置在钢筋上,然后将钢筋巧妙地伪装起来。演员飘在"树枝"上或"鸟儿"上,让观众倍感惊奇。

Piao-se is a fusion of opera, acrobatics and decorative arts. It features a little child standing on a small piece of board, which is put on some corrugated steel bars; and these steel bars then bear a smart camouflage. Performers thus drift on tree branches or birds, exciting audience.

龙舟竞渡
Dragon Boat Competition

龙舟竞渡在广州至少有上千年的历史。早期赛龙舟只是一种宫廷活动,到明、清时演变为群众性的活动。1995年起,广州每年都举办国际龙舟邀请赛。数十条龙舟在珠江上奋勇争先,盛况空前。

A over-1,000-year-old event in Guangzhou. Initially, such an event was held within the imperial palace only. Later in Ming and Qing Dynasties, it prevailed in the multitude. Since 1995, Guangzhou has started to launch an International Dragon Boat Invitation Competition on an annual basis. Dozens of dragon boats competing against one another at full speed, constitute an exciting scene.

民俗风情

粤剧
Guangdong Opera

我国南方一大剧种，流行于广东、广西及港澳、东南亚等地，唱念均用广州方言。它以"梆簧"为基本曲调，同时又保留昆、戈、广腔并吸收广东民间乐曲和时调。伴奏除了民族乐器外大胆地采用西洋乐器，表演和舞美吸收了其他艺术的长处，形成了自己的特色。著名演员有马师曾、红线女等。

A major kind of opera in China's south, prevailing in Guangdong province, Guangxi province, HK, Macao, and Southeastern countries. Performed in the dialect of Guangzhou: Cantonese. It employs "Bang-Huang" as the basic tone, and has also preserved the folk melodies and tunes of Kunqu Opera, Ge opera and Guang opera. As to accompaniments, it boldly uses musical instruments of different nationalities and even western musical instruments. In terms of stage designing and performance, it has also absorbed the good points of other operas too, further gaining its own characteristics. Famed performers of Guangdong opera include Ma Shi-zeng and Red-bandeau Lady, etc.

私伙局
Folk Arts Center

广州热心曲艺戏剧表演者众多，有专业的也有业余的。他们暇闲时，或在自家宅中，或公共场所里自娱自乐，演奏演唱广东音乐、曲艺和粤剧，俗称为私伙局。图为在人民公园中常见的私伙局娱乐活动。

Guangzhou has housed a great number of opera lovers; among them, some are professional players, while others are amateur players. In leisure times, they perform operas either at home or in public areas. The picture shows a snapshot of the performing scene in the People's Park.

岭南艺术

广彩
Guangzhou Colorized Ceramics

广彩又叫广州织金彩瓷,生产过程为描线、填色、织金、填绿、斗彩、包金口、烧花等工序。成品色鲜明绚丽,是我国釉上彩瓷的一个独特的品种。
Colorized ceramics are made by a series of production links, such as line drawing, color filing, etc. Finished products of colorized ceramics feature sharp colors, constituting a special variety.

广雕
Guangzhou Style Sculpture

广雕中的象牙雕以精雕细刻著称,象牙球可雕45层,层层活动;玉雕历史源远流长,有"留色"特技;木雕是传统民间工艺,玲珑剔透,十分精湛。
The ivory sculpture of Guangzhou style features exquisite craftsmanship; an ivory ball can host up to 45 layers, each of which can move freely. The jade sculpting techniques emerged in China a rather long period of time ago; while "color preservation" technology has been known as a technical know-how. Wood sculpting has also been a traditional branch of folk arts, featuring great craftsmanship, too.

岭南艺术

广绣
Guangzhou Style Embroidery

广绣以色彩鲜明、形象生动著称,与苏绣、湘绣、蜀绣并称为全国"四大 名绣"。在历史上广绣多作为朝廷贡品,故宫现存的绣品中有不少广绣精品。
Guangzhou style embroidery features sharp colors and true-to-life figures, and is listed as one of the four major embroidery genres in China (the other three are Suzhou style one, Hunan style one and Sichuan style one). In China's history, most embroidery pieces of Guangzhou style have been used as articles of tribute to the imperial palaces. Many of the embroidery pieces collected within the Imperial Palace in today's Beijing are of Guangzhou style.

广州艺术博物院
Guangzhou Arts Museum

位于麓湖路,是华南地区最大的艺术类博物馆。该院的收藏以中国历代书画作品为基础,特别是以岭南地区的书画作品为重点,兼顾其他门类的历代艺术品。藏品年代上起新石器时代,下至当代,其中不少为国宝级文物,具有很高的艺术价值和历史价值。

Nestled in Lu-hu Road, known as the largest arts museum of its kind in South China region. Engaged in collecting Chinese calligraphy and painting works of past generations, with a focus on those works of Ling-nan (the south of the Five Ridges, i.e. the area covering Guangdong and Guangxi provinces); other types of historical artworks were also collected into the museum. Among the artworks in the museum, some could date back to the Neolithic age, others are contemporary masterpieces; and many of them are highly precious treasures, and of significant values in artistic and historical terms.

红线女艺术中心
Red-bandeau Lady Arts Center

位于珠江新城,是广州市政府为表彰红线女对中华优秀文化艺术的卓越贡献而投资兴建的。红线女创造了享誉海内外的"红派"艺术,她所塑造的舞台形象,在粤剧史上留下绚丽篇章,红线女的艺术代表着当代粤剧旦角艺术的最高成就,被誉为岭南文化瑰宝。

Nestled in the Pearl River New City, initially established by the City Government of Guangzhou to commend the great contributions made by an outstanding female performer of Guangdong opera, usually called Red-bandeau Lady. She created a globally famed "Red style" performing art, and has been considered as the most successful female player of Guangdong opera so far.

岭南艺术

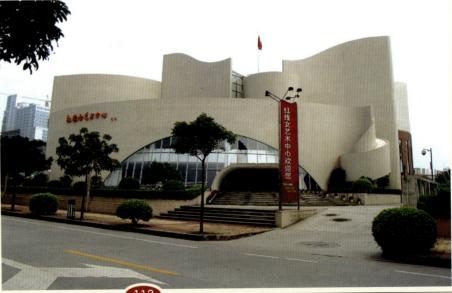

广东美术馆
Guangdong Ar Gallery

位于二沙岛，是按现代多功能目标规划建设的造型艺术博物馆。该馆有十二个展览厅和户外雕塑展示区，可举办各种大型展览；以中国近现代以来的美术作品和海外华人美术作品为收藏对象，以中国近现代沿海美术和广东当代美术为收藏重点。
Nestled in Er-sha Island, known as a multi-functional plastic arts museum. Hosts 12 exhibition halls and an outdoor sculpture exhibition area, able to house various kinds of large-sized exhibition events. Engaged in collecting those latter-day artistic works in China and those artistic works of overseas Chinese, with a focus on those artistic works emerging in coastal regions in the latter-day China and especially those artistic works in today's Guangdong.

岭南艺术

星海音乐厅
Xing-hai Concert Hall

位于二沙岛，其交响乐演奏厅是目前国内最大的纯自然声演奏厅，其声学指标是按国际"顶级"要求设计的，舞台装有亚洲目前最大的巨型管风琴，观众席共1500座位；其室内乐演奏厅具有国际水平，共460座位。
Nestled in Er-sha Island; the symphony hall in here is the country's biggest unplugged performance hall, with its acoustical indicators measuring up to the "first-rate" standards acknowledged by the international community. The stage is installed with the largest pipe organ in today's Asia. The seating capacity is 1,500 persons; the indoor performance hall has measured up to the international standard, with 460 seats in total.

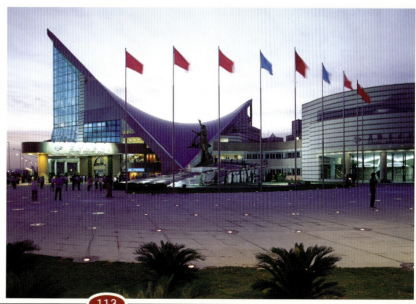

广州老字号
Time-honored shops in Guangzhou

广州的老字号发展历史悠久,见证了广州工商业文化兴旺发达的历史,其中有很多不但在国内,而且在海外都还很有名气。老字号蕴藏着丰富的历史文化信息,代表着广州的形象和文化底蕴。本版选图为部分广州比较著名的老字号酒家。广州的老字号酒家在建筑布局和店堂装饰上都有鲜明的岭南特色,在饮食文化上有重要的贡献,是"食在广州"的重要诠释者。上图为陶陶居,中图为莲香楼,下左图为北园酒家,下右图为广州酒家。

Guangzhou has hosted a number of time-honored shops each with a solid reputation, which have witnessed the boom and prosperity in the business community in the city. Some of these shops have enjoyed a wholesome fame not only at home, but also abroad. We have selected a galaxy of renowned restaurants in Guangzhou, which feature eye-catching characteristics in terms of interior decoration, architectural layout and cuisine presentation. The upper picture shows Tao-tao-ju Restaurant, the middle picture shows Lian-xiang-lou Restaurant, the lower picture on the left shows Bei-yuan restaurant, and the lower picture on the right shows Guangzhou Restaurant.

老字号

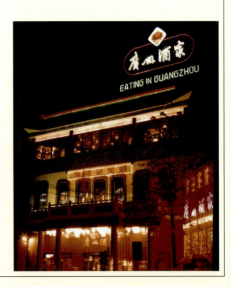